WITHDRAWN

IN CELEBRATION OF SMALL THINGS

A SAN FRANCISCO BOOK COMPANY / HOUGHTON MIFFLIN BOOK

Houghton Mifflin Company   Boston   1974

Sharon Cadwallader

In Celebration of Small Things

ILLUSTRATED BY ANITA WALKER SCOTT

Printed in the United States of America

This SAN FRANCISCO BOOK COMPANY / HOUGHTON MIFFLIN BOOK originated in San Francisco and was produced and published jointly. Distribution is by Houghton Mifflin Company, 2 Park Street, Boston, Massachusetts 02107.

Library of Congress Cataloging in Publication Data

Cadwallader, Sharon.
    In celebration of small things.

    "A San Francisco Book Company/Houghton Mifflin book."
    Includes bibliographies.
    1. Home economics.   I. Title.
TX145.C126   640   73–23002
ISBN 0–395–17213–6   ISBN 0–913374–08–3
ISBN 0–395–18092–9 (pbk.)   ISBN 0–913374–09–1 (pbk.)

The author is grateful for permission to reprint the following lines:
    From the book *Winnie-the-Pooh* by A. A. Milne; decorations by E. H. Shepard: Copyright, 1926, by E. P. Dutton & Co., Inc. New York, renewal, 1954, by A. A. Milne. Published by E. P. Dutton & Co., Inc., New York, and used with their permission; with permission also of McClelland and Stewart, Ltd., Toronto, and of Methuen and Company, Ltd., London.
    From the song "Into White" by Cat Stevens: Copyright 1970, Freshwater Music, Ltd. (England) Controlled in the Western Hemisphere by Irving Music, Inc. (BMI) All Rights Reserved. Used by Permission.

Contents

For my MOTHER *and* FATHER

Introduction

THIS BOOK is a call for the celebration of human resourcefulness and creativity.

With the emergence of technological assistance in this century, much of the daily toil necessary for survival in the past has been eliminated by machinery, leaving people in the western world an unprecedented amount of free time. My concern in writing this book is the price we are paying for that free time, for it appears to me that we are losing valuable skills and talents as we cease to do things for ourselves. And I believe the question of our usefulness to ourselves and to each other should determine the design of tomorrow's lifestyles.

I am certainly not alone in my concern. The last decade in the United States has brought many changes in the life patterns of a large segment of Americans, and new attitudes toward responsibility are emerging from the understanding that we must not surrender to the button and the lever of industrial society. Especially strong among the younger generations is the feeling that we must restore the acts and rituals of doing for ourselves in order to maintain control over how we live. It is not possible, however, for us to renounce the industrial revolution; we cannot all return to the land for total subsistence or make for ourselves all the necessities of life. So for most of us the answer lies in creating a balance, in developing a self-sufficiency that is *harmonious* with the best gifts of technology. Having grown up in Southern California and having lived in rural and small communities since then, I feel the answer lies somewhere between Los Angeles and Walden Pond. This book is a statement of that belief.

There are ten chapters in the book, each containing a variety of suggestions for enriching everyday life. The first chapters offer inexpensive, resourceful, and creative suggestions for the home and immediate neighborhood, while the last four chapters contain thoughts about the community, environmental responsibilities, and festivities. Many of these ideas are actually variations on customs and habits of the past; in this book I am working to build more bridges between that early American ingenuity and the sophistication of contemporary living.

Each reader should establish his or her priorities and interests to determine where to start reading. Not all of the content will appeal to every reader; nor will everyone be able to use each idea in every environment. We all have different areas of capability and different degrees of involvement in family and community life. Some chapters present ideas on which to build and improvise; others include detailed directions that should be followed carefully. Most of all, I hope the total concept of the book will lead the reader to his or her own thoughts, plans, and dreams.

Chapter 1 is a starting point in the home. Because its purpose is to create an image of simple transformation in the reader's mind, it is written as an essay without much detailed instruction. It is a general guide to changing any modern kitchen into a warm gathering place, a food studio for everyone. Some of the other chapters contain specific how-to instructions for the suggestions in Chapter 1.

Chapter 2 is about food gardening in containers. Although there is much interest today in raising fruits and vegetables, little has been written for those who do not have land but do have space for containers. The information is complete for the subject, but for those who do have a small plot of land, there are several good books recommended at the end of the chapter.

Chapter 3 is a thorough explanation of the art of preserving. I grew up with preserving as an important part of my own home life and have tried to include here all the tricks I have learned over the years.

Chapter 4 is a touch of luxury. Home brewing and winemaking are popular activities now, and these beer and wine recipes are easy, inexpensive, and delicious. The instructions in this chapter are sufficient for the recipes contained, and for those who would like more variety (especially in winemaking), there are, again, a number of helpful books suggested at the end of the chapter.

Chapters 5 and 6 are personal testimonies to the ease of sewing, decorating, building, and repairing in the home. These are things my family, my friends, and I have done in our homes; they are ideas that have received responses like: "How did you do it?"; "What a great idea!"; "Is that really easy?"; and "That gives me an idea." I hope by using these simple suggestions the reader will gain the confidence to invent more complicated projects. I am certain that almost everyone will find something in these chapters that will appeal to his or her taste or talent. The second part of Chapter 6 covers some common repairs in the home. From my own experience of living in old dwellings, I have selected problems that seem to occur most often, as I know only too well what the cost can be for even the most elementary malfunction when we hire a plumber or an electrician. My father, while he could ride a horse like a cowboy, play the harmonica sitting on a fencepost, and make wonderful sourdough pancakes, was not too handy with the screwdriver. My mother, on the other hand, was challenged by every mechanical obstinacy and could fix nearly everything that went wrong in our house. My fix-it ability lies somewhere between my two parents. For those more talented than I, there are reading lists for these chapters that will help the reader master some of the more intricate crafts and devilish repairs.

Chapters 7, 8, and 9 shift the focus from home to community. Chapter 7 is a commentary on the problems of shopping in today's supermarkets, with aisle-by-aisle advice on how to buy more health and less nonsense with today's food dollar. Chapter 8 is a fairly detailed discussion of environmental problems, both immediate and long range. It offers a variety of suggestions about eliminating waste in our everyday lives, as well as in the larger environment. Chapter 9 centers around the immediate community with many suggestions for the revival of a cooperative spirit among people living in the same geographical area. Within this section are a number of new and old ideas for improving community relations through co-operative businesses, recreational projects, exchanges of skills and labor, and community festivities.

Chapter 10 is a call for both the reevaluation and creation of meaningful rituals and commemorative moments in modern life.

I think we all have the desire and capacity to develop better management of the small energies that make up domestic living. We all have *more* personal talent to unleash and more concern for the people and earth around us than we have found ways to express in these technological times. I am certain that simplifying the *everyday* with skill and meaning provides the basis for developing an understanding of the broad issues that face a large, industrial society. And the refinement and integration of both levels in ourselves is the commitment to becoming citizens who can provide a dignified and humane future for our country.

Sharon Cadwallader

Santa Cruz, California
October 1973

CHAPTER 1

Welcome to
the Country Kitchen

After the supper and talk—after the day is done,

As a friend from friends his final withdrawal prolonging . . .

WALT WHITMAN, *After the Supper and Talk*

THE COUNTRY KITCHEN is not indigenous to America, but it certainly is as old as the seeds of independence. The houses constructed by the colonists in New England, known as saltboxes, were generally built with two rooms first. The larger main room was called the common room, a kind of kitchen-living room that functioned as the hub of the house. No matter how many rooms were added on, the common room remained the center of the home. Cooking was done in and over the fireplace, which was very large, as it was the only source of heat. Later, brick ovens were built into the fireplaces for roasting and baking.

These large family rooms were thick with activity. The women did all their sewing, weaving, spinning, dyeing, and candlemaking in the warmth of the common room. Children played or studied and the baby's cradle remained near the hearth day and night. At the end of the day's work, the men gathered around the table to discuss local politics and problems. In the evening, both young and old sat on benches in the warm corner of the hearth while the head of the household read from the Bible. It was not uncommon for the master and mistress to sleep in the common room, and quite often the young children slept in a trundle bed which was stored under their parents' bed during the day. It was not until much later, in city houses, that food preparation was moved to a special room separate from the dining and entertaining area. Even then the kitchen remained a gathering spot for all the servants.

Indeed, the country kitchen is American. Wherever new settlements were formed the initial structures began with and centered around kitchen-living areas. The concept was implicit in the architecture: a beginning, a nucleus, always a common gathering place where the family could gather alone or with friends to eat, exchange news, and discuss future plans.

Prior to central heating, the kitchen, large or small, offered the necessary warmth to draw the family in the morning and evening. Even on the midwestern prairies, where fireplaces were rare because of the scarcity of wood, the kitchen stove, stoked with soft coal, was kept burning all day in the cold months while doors to other rooms remained closed to prevent drafts. If the kitchen and dining area were one, there was often a separate summer kitchen with a kerosene stove, which did not emit heat as a wood-burning stove did. Or, in some instances, houses contained separate dining rooms where the family could escape the heat of the cookstove during the hot months. The living room or parlor usually contained a coal-burning heating stove, but such rooms were used only for company or special occasions.

Unfortunately, the last forty years of American life have witnessed some drastic changes in kitchen space and function. Affluence and changing social patterns made the dining room the proper place for main meals. Kitchen eating became socially less acceptable and, once finished with its meal, the family dispersed to other areas of the house. The living room became the social gathering spot, the place for the radio and subsequently the television. Thus, the idea of the kitchen as a center remained largely in the lower classes.

Then, after World War II, with the enormous birthrate among young marrieds, huge tract home developments built for resale and aimed at middle-income families began to appear all over the United States. A maturing of floor plans and the demand for more living space, compounded possibly by the growing concern and anxiety over the decentralization of larger postwar families, gave birth to the kitchen-family room combination. But, regrettably, in most of these newer homes, the actual kitchen area is very small and sterile, with little more than a cubicle or counter where food is handed through a space that resembles a service window in a hamburger stand.

It is curious, too, that domestic and commercial foods have become so similar. All over America thousands of quick-lunch stands make it possible to get a meal made from precooked, prepared, nutritionless products in minutes. In supermarkets, frozen, prepared jiffy breakfast, lunch, and dinner foods have become major stock for the American kitchen. One can drive to the store, select dinner ingredients and, with some quick preparation, finish the whole plastic process in as little as three-quarters of an hour (providing the checkout line is not too long). Quite a change from the time when preparation for the evening meal began after breakfast and there was stirring, kneading, and shaping throughout the day.

Well, given the cultural and industrial changes in our society in the first half of this century, the image of a woman spending the entire day washing, ironing, mending, and fixing the evening meal is not likely to regain popularity. On the other hand, a growing concern about the quality of food consumed by the average American today and a gnawing awareness of the degeneration of the family group necessitate a look toward alternatives to our present family life-styles.

I suggest we start with a return to the American country kitchen. Let's exchange the food laboratory for the food studio. We all accept the indisputable advantage of gas and electricity in today's home. Stoking the fire in the stove throughout the day and running outside in the rain or snow to the root cellar are among the many chores that no longer absorb one's time and energy. But there is a limit to the validity of labor-saving devices. Many sterile, unattractive kitchen gadgets can be eliminated with no loss of convenience or efficiency, and the avoidance, even rejection, of these items is advantageous on two levels. First, it would make a small, but definite, commitment to the conservation of power; and second, it would help restore a deeply needed aestheticism to food preparation. With so much precooked, processed food being used today, and with so many shortcuts and so many items available for speedy preparation, I feel a decadence emerging in our lives. We have dissociated the means of creating from the end product. In cooking, as in any creative form, attention must be given to the total cycle of creation to produce beautiful, healthful results. This cycle, if reinstated, will have everyone wanting to get into the creative act by questioning, commenting, smelling, tasting, and stirring. And such continuing appreciation will serve as an emotional stimulant for the woman who wants to move into new forms of creativity in her kitchen-studio.

It is difficult to make the commitment to an emotional and functional change in the isolated coldness of the present-day American kitchen, but any kitchen, large or small, can be turned into a studio with a bit of imagination and determination.

After removing some of the superfluous electrical extras (who knows what all the electrical energy passing through the room does to your psyche), you will find you can replace these items with small, inexpensive hand-operated items that take less space. Coffee made in a good old-fashioned drip pot from beans ground fresh each time in a small, inexpensive hand coffee grinder is a great asset to socializing in the kitchen. It is important to mention here, though, that everyone has different cooking techniques and food preferences that are the result of many years of habits. Some items drawing electrical energy may be very important to you, so don't discard them and sacrifice all convenience. It's a matter of priorities. I have an electrical incubator for yogurt and I do appreciate its uniform heating system. The blender is a terrific invention and some of the newer ones have a button that operates only so long as you touch it, which is, I think, a small power and noise saver. I like sourdough waffles, so I keep a waffle iron instead of a toaster and make toast in the oven. Figure out what is really important to you and recycle the rest to people who need and can use them. Consider the aged and the handicapped, or institutions where there is a flow of people and a shortage of labor. There are people and places who could use that electric knife sharpener or can opener.

Let's go to the windows. So many homes and apartments now have aluminum-sashed windows. While they may be tight and easy to open, I think they are rather cold. The type of curtain you use in your kitchen (if you use a curtain) will make a lot of difference in the warmth of a window, but one idea which is both fun and beautiful is to glue a design made of little pieces of broken glass on the window glass. It obscures any not-too-pleasant view and adds color and warmth. My kitchen window in Mexico was very attractive in its basic form. It was right above the sink, recessed with tile, with many small panes and rimmed with wrought iron, and it opened inward. The action in the village street was fascinating to watch through bowls of ripening tropical fruit and fresh roses from the garden sitting on the sill. It made truly a wonderful image as I cleaned vegetables and washed dishes. But a former occupant had added a perfect touch to the window with a sunburst design on one pane, shining with those rich colors found in Mexican glassware. The pieces were firmly secured with an epoxy glue that dries clear. Or, you can edge a window with small pieces of broken glass, which enhance the view and light rays. This is a wonderful way to use the mellow color tones of broken beer and wine bottles. For those who have small windows looking down backstairs or fire escapes, it is nice to glue rice paper on the panes. This eliminates uninteresting scenes yet permits light. I have used rice paper on bathroom windows for privacy, without sacrificing light. Also, if you can reach out the kitchen window, you can hang a small washtub herb garden in front of the window (outside). Use a large outdoor hook from the hardware store, but make certain you can water and snip your herbs and that they get some sun. See the section on raising herbs in Chapter 2.

The window sill is a special place. I have a small window over my sink that gets a lot of afternoon sun. To utilize the rays, I put small colored bottles of seeds on the middle ledge, and larger bottles of

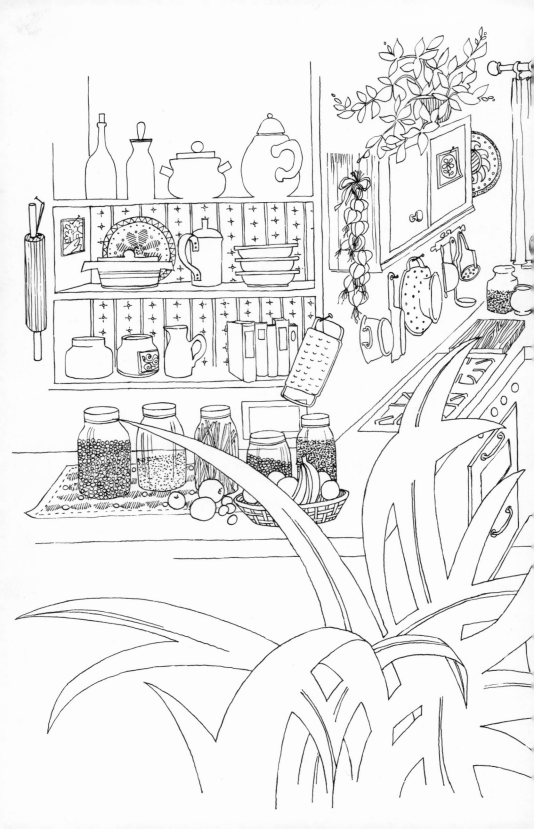

dried herbs, weeds, and chopsticks on the lower sill. (Chapter 3 contains suggestions for drying foods as a form of preserving.) The sun through the various glass bottles (I have to remember to dust) is the first image one catches when entering the kitchen.

The window sill is also a place for small plants. In fact, the kitchen is definitely a place for growing things. There are excellent little house plants that do well in the heat of the kitchen. English ivy is attractive, although it really likes cooler air, so put it by an open window or the refrigerator (actually, I have a little ivy plant on a shelf by my stove and it is healthy enough, although it hasn't grown as well as the one in a window draft).

One nice way to add living things to your kitchen is to root vegetables and plant fruit seeds. The avocado and sweet potato are common kitchen plants. Soak an avocado pit in water until the skin can be removed easily. Secure three toothpicks in the middle of the pit to balance it in a jar or glass of water. Half of the seed (point end) should be out of the water and the other half submerged. Keep the water at a constant level and the seed in a light but not-too-sunny spot. It will take a few weeks for the seed to split and sprout. After a few days of sprouting, transplant it into a pot of earth or potting soil and watch it grow into a beautiful plant. It helps to feed it fish emulsion occasionally. This fertilizer is a good food for most house plants, as well as small container gardens of vegetables.

Sprouting a sweet potato is even easier. Use the same method as with the avocado pit without presoaking. It will sprout fast, but it should stay out of the direct light until it is well sprouted. Devise a basket arrangement of twine and beads for hanging the jar. The growing shoots can be trained to wind around the twine, and if you do not allow too many shoots to grow, the others will have thick foliage.

Sprigs of ivy, which are lovely anywhere in the house, can also be rooted in water. Use a narrow-neck bottle like a wine bottle. Beet and carrot tops will grow more shoots if you leave a few inches of the vegetable in moist sand or water. Plant well-washed citrus seeds in potting soil rich in sand and watch them sprout into pretty plants. It's easy to keep your kitchen full of green, growing things.

If you don't like the slick quality of your stove and refrigerator, or if they must be in a bad spot and seem to loom out, there are several ways you can minimize the problem. To paint flowers or designs on the door and sides of the refrigerator, all you need is a good enamel paint. A stove demands paint which is resistant to high heat, and this is especially necessary for older stoves that are not well insulated and become very hot to touch. Heat-resistant paints come in spray containers and cannot be brushed on because they dry so fast, but it is easy to make designs on your stove if you first cut a stencil and spray your various colors carefully.

If there is room on your stove, add a tall basket for cooking utensils. There is nothing better than a good assortment of wooden spoons for stirring. Baskets are a warm, earthy addition to the country kitchen, and you can often pick them up for very little at flea markets and rummage sales. Use them for oranges, lemons, potatoes, onions, and cloth napkins. A long French bread basket is perfect for knives. I favor hanging kitchen items for handy use. Anywhere there is wood for nailing, I hang pots, pans, colanders, strainers, measuring spoons, cups, and cleavers. Fill your window rims with these objects and cover the wall with prints, paintings, photographs, and old mirrors. Make a food collage of pictures cut from magazines or old cookbooks. Favorite recipes written on fabric make good hangings. A staple gun is useful for putting up prints and posters.

If you live in a rented apartment or house where there are rules about putting nails in the walls, especially when they are made from sheetrock, which does not hold nails well, get a large piece of pegboard from the lumber yard and secure it with molly bolts made especially for this purpose. Spacers are also sold with the pegboard, through which the screws are attached to the wall. The spacers hold the pegboard out from the wall so that hooks can be slipped into the peg holes and you can hang everything on one board.

Many apartments today have formica counters in the kitchen,

which may be practical, but they tend to give a cold overall effect. With no harm to the counters or permanent change to the basic structure, you can easily build an inexpensive oak cutting board that will fit over the counter. (For building instructions, see Chapter 6.) The effect is both aesthetic and functional.

Another hint for warming up the kitchen is to display colorful cookware and glasses on open shelves. You can either remove the doors and hinges from a cupboard, or build simple shelves from pine or redwood. (For building instructions, see Chapter 6.) I have an extra cupboard made from pine in my kitchen that I use for jars of grains, nuts, pasta, and dried fruits. Many decorator jars are sold for displaying foodstuffs, but it is more economical to go around to large local restaurants and bars and get their glass containers from olives, onions, cherries, and other condiments. Generally, restaurant people are very happy to give them away. Sometimes delicatessens have large jars left over from pickles and pigs' feet. Save all your vitamin and small condiment jars for dried herbs. Paint the lids (outside only) and use gummed labels for identification. Be sure you display your home preserves too! Why should we hide good natural foods in closed cupboards? A painter in his studio does not hide his paints or brushes, nor a sculptor his materials or tools.

Much has been said about the current movement toward independence for women in many fields, from business and government to education and marriage. What is commonly forgotten, however, is that the point to women's liberation is to remove unnatural barriers that have restricted growth and development. Left alone to explore personal interests through random research, unstructured reading, or exposure to the arts, all of us, men *and* women, need a place at home where everything is possible and nothing denied.

If the kitchen is large enough, for example, the studio idea can be expanded. It is a perfect place for a piano or sewing machine, a loom or a library table, bookcase, reading chairs or a couch, and of course a large table in trestle, round, or mission-plank style, where everyone can gather, eat, and talk.

I do all my writing in the kitchen. I wrote *Whole Earth Cook Book* there, and my sister typed the manuscript at the desk in her kitchen. My neighbor, a creative country-kitchen type, has an alcove in her kitchen where she sews. These arrangements enable you to cook while sewing, reading, writing, painting, or socializing. There are endless personal varieties of country kitchens that one can develop.

The compartmentalization of American life has had an inhibiting effect on the woman in her own home, so that her creativity has been channeled away from her work area. But just as her family's health can be reclaimed through attention to better foods, so should her own kitchen-studio be reclaimed so that she can explore all levels of her talent. In this way, all of us can gather once again in our common rooms for good, healthful food, rich conversation, and a general inclusive family warmth.

CHAPTER 2

Starting a
Container Garden

A little too abstract, a little too wise,

It is time for us to kiss the earth again.

ROBINSON JEFFERS, *Return*

ONE SATISFYING activity in which people all over the country can participate is home gardening. In fact, the return to food gardening in the last few years in the United States is a significant commentary on the interest in more resourceful living. Most gardeners of the organic method are part of the growing reaction to commercial, chemical gardening. Not since the Victory Gardens of the Second World War has so much collective spirit arisen for raising vegetables and fruit, and never before in this country have there been the community support and exchange of gardening ideas we see today (see Chapter 9).

A great deal has been published in recent years on the values and techniques of organic farming methods for the home gardener or small farmer. Unfortunately, many city and suburban apartment dwellers feel excluded from these projects, though they may be concerned about food pollution. Except in special gardening publications with limited circulation, there is little information available on container vegetable gardening, although the interest in such activity is growing. Therefore, the vegetable gardening ideas and instructions in this chapter are addressed to those individuals who, although they have not even a border of earth for cultivating, do have a balcony, an accessible rooftop, an atrium, or a sometimes-sunny porch. Roof gardens are not uncommon in the cities, and we see many balconies nowadays with flowers and plants thriving. The old-time window box is still a familiar sight in ethnic areas. Yet the possibility of making a salad from the contents of these container gardens is a new idea to many. I hope in time it will become a common practice. All instructions and suggestions given here are the result of experimenting under just such conditions with the adjustments that are required.

For those who have small plots of land around their houses, or are fortunate to be in a community that has developed areas for community gardening plots (see Chapter 9), a good list of gardening books is included at the end of this chapter.

Planning Your Area

Summer vegetables and herbs need sun, although some require and benefit from less direct sun and cooler weather than others. Judge your area carefully in relation to size and light conditions. If you have a reasonably large porch, balcony, or rooftop area, you will be able to grow a good variety of vegetables, but if confined to a fairly small area with limited sun, you will get the best results by raising hearty greens and lettuce and perhaps pole beans and tomatoes. Each of these will give you a high yield for the space because you can cut back their outer leaves and the plants will continue to replenish themselves. If you have a limited amount of direct sunlight, but can create good soil conditions, it would be wise to try some root vegetables such as onions, carrots, and radishes. Measure your area and begin to consider the type of planter that would best fit.

Choosing Planters

There are a number of types of planters to make, round up, or buy that will work well for this garden plan. I prefer redwood planters as they are durable, pleasantly rough hewn, cheap and easy to make, and the old standby terra-cotta pots which range in size from 2 to 14 inches in diameter. Narrow planters have two properties to consider: they are easy to build and they prevent creating a container of too much weight.

18

Nearly every nursery in the country carries redwood planters of different varieties and sizes. If your handiest nursery does not, it probably will order them for you or refer you to a place that does carry them. Considering the possibility of a lack of tools, the difficulty of carrying lumber on the subway or bus, and your having little skill in carpentry, the instructions for these planter boxes are designed to compete with the easiest "do-it-yourself kit" on the market.

FIVE-FOOT PLANTER (*Approximate cost: $4.00*)

Materials needed: 3 pieces 6-foot × 12-inch × 1-inch
                    rough-sawn redwood
                    1 pound 6d galvanized nails
                    10-point hand saw
                    hammer

1. Cut the lumber as shown.

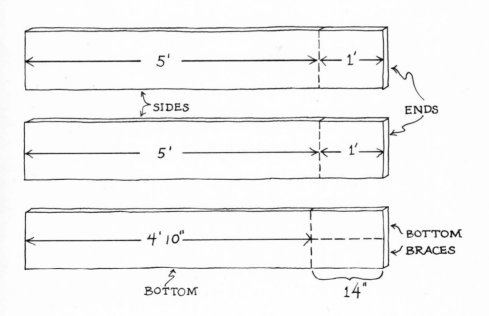

2. Cut three 1-inch triangular notches for drainage on each side of the 4-foot–10-inch piece. Avoid knots.

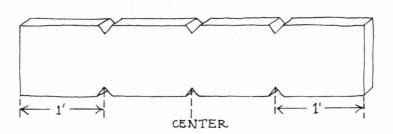

3. Square off one end piece to bottom piece and pound in three nails.

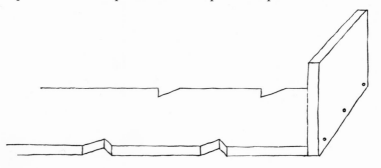

4. Attach side piece to end and bottom. Continue with other end and final side.

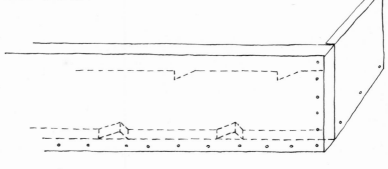

5. Nail 14-inch strips underneath to brace and elevate for drainage (or attach casters).
   Don't nail over notches.

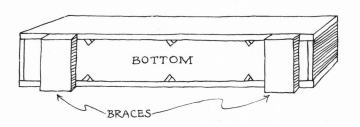

TWO–FOOT PLANTER (*Approximate cost: $2.00*)

Materials needed: 1 8-foot × 12-inch × 1-inch piece
rough-sawn redwood
6d galvanized nails
10-point hand saw
hammer

Cut as shown:

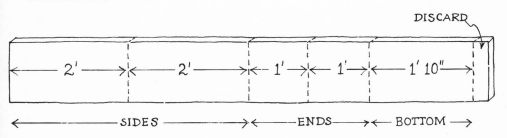

Notch bottom and follow same procedure as for larger planter. Use casters or bricks to elevate for drainage.

Drainage is a crucial factor for the apartment garden. Clay pots all have trays which work well for this purpose. With the redwood

21

planters, the casters or wooden braces are to raise them for drainage and facilitate moving them in and out of the sun. Good soil will not drain like a sieve anyway, and the casters or braces will work well if you place ice cube trays, cut-off milk cartons, or any similar receptacle under all drainage holes. If the soil is good and you water more frequently and less intensely, drainage will not be profuse.

Other receptacles will also work well for planting. Coffee cans and plastic cartons are fine if you punch good drainage holes. Bushel baskets, small barrels, or even most wooden crates or boxes are usable, but remember that they will need to be coated inside with creosote or an anti-rot preparation as they will not withstand moisture like redwood.

Soil Preparation

In my experiments, the best crops have come from soil combinations that are at least half good rich topsoil or garden loam. Most commercial planter mixes, while adequate for house plants already into their growing stage, do not contain enough nutrients to bring the vegetables to their final stage of development. I recommend finding a good source of natural soil to mix half and half with planter mix. If you are certain that your supply of natural soil is truly rich, you can lessen the total weight in the planter by mixing one-fourth vermiculite and one-fourth perlite. The first is a decomposition of rock and the other a light form of volcanic ash. It is difficult to prescribe an absolute soil combination to be used nationwide. Confer with a local nursery or vegetable gardener about the available soil and planter mixes in your area. Soil laboratories throughout the country are continuously experimenting with various mixes for nurseries and home gardeners.

If you do use my suggestion of soil and planter mix, sow the seeds directly in the planters to avoid damaging the seedlings in the process of transplanting. In areas where frosts linger you can buy individual seedling peat pots to be used to start the seeds. These pots are made from compressed peat moss and can be filled with soil or soil and planter mix, but plant no more than three seeds per pot.

When the seedlings develop two sets of leaves or more, simply thin them to the strongest single plant and sink the plant, peat pot and all, into the soil of your permanent container. The roots grow right through the peat container, which disintegrates as the plants grow.

Seedlings should not be fertilized as young plants cannot accept a concentration of nutrients and will shrivel up. Do not add any fertilizer until the plants have reached a height of 4 to 5 inches. Then select a fertilizer with your nursery clerk and follow the directions carefully for the amount and frequency. A good, mild, all-around fertilizer is fish emulsion, which can be purchased in any nursery. It works well on all vegetables, and if you buy young tomato plants it can be applied directly after you have transplanted them into the permanent containers.

Mixing the Soil

If you have an old tub, use it to mix your soil combination. Moisten as you mix to keep the dust down. The mixture settles as it becomes damp, so it is important to get it nicely damp before transferring it to the planters.

If you aren't using casters, first place your planters where you want them and make the drainage arrangements. Then move the soil to the planters (large, full planters can become very heavy). Mix several batches to fill the larger planter. To help with drainage, it is a good idea to put a layer of coarse sand on the bottom of the planter before putting in the soil mixture.

Choosing Your Crop

The selection of vegetables depends on the size and number of planters and on your own taste. Remember that leafy vegetables will give a higher yield per area, but you may want to try a few root vegetables too.

Seeds

Seed racks are found in nurseries, in hardware stores and, very commonly, in markets. The seeds you select should be acclimated to

23

your geographical area and packaged for the season in which you are growing. It is wise to consult the nursery people in your area for advice on which brand they recommend. Experiments are always being made in the seed field and special strains are developed for certain climate and soil conditions. My friends and I on the West Coast prefer Burpee seeds, but there are many good companies.

CARROTS: Home-grown carrots are so delicious you will certainly want to try growing some. I suggest either the midget variety, which matures most quickly, or the short, fat type, which is very tasty. The longer carrots may present a problem unless your planters are good and deep. Sow early in spring, and when the seedlings get to be 1 to 1½ inches tall, thin them to about 1 inch apart. Then, after a month or so, thin them to about 3 inches apart. Incidentally, you can enjoy the sweet taste of these tiny thinnings in salad. Generally it will take eight to ten weeks for full maturity.

RADISHES: Both carrots and radishes can take an early sowing. Radishes grow beautifully in these soil combinations and should be eaten as soon as they are mature because they quickly get dry and pithy. Thin them to an inch apart after they are about 2 inches tall, and they should be ready to eat in a month, or earlier. When you pull a radish, replace it with another seed and start a second crop.

ONIONS AND SHALLOTS: Sow seeds very early in spring. Even better, start onions and shallots (the delicate little bulb that is a cross between onion and garlic and is used in French cooking) with "sets," very young plants that are available at nurseries. Separate the sets and plant an inch apart, and the bulbs will be ready to eat in a month to six weeks. When an onion top falls, it's time to pull the onion; then let it dry in the sun for several days to a week. Ask your nursery clerk for specific directions on the variety you choose. Green onions will be ready to eat faster because you are eating the shoots before they form large bulbs.

BEETS AND TURNIPS: These are very good for planters as you can eat both the root and the greens. Sow early in the spring and when the plants have grown to about 1½ to 2 inches, thin them to 1½

24

inches apart. Thin again when they have reached a height of 7 to 8 inches. They are best when young, so don't let them get larger than 2 inches in diameter.

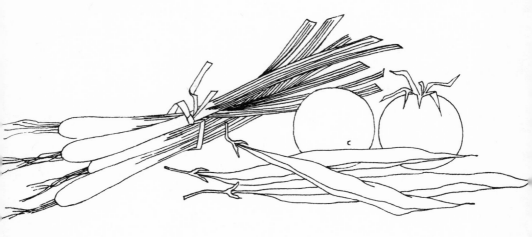

SWISS CHARD AND SPINACH: Swiss chard is usually much better as a summer crop than spinach, which does not flourish in hot weather. One exception is New Zealand spinach, an extraordinarily hearty variety that will grow and spread for months. Young tips can be picked throughout the summer months. Chop fine for salads and cook longer than ordinary spinach, for this plant is tougher. It is also considered to be more nutritious. A vinelike quality makes New Zealand spinach a good hanging plant.

KALE: This plant is new to most people, or known only as cattle food. It is well worth growing because it has the heartiness of a weed and grows all year in many areas. Treat it as you would any green, but pick it young and discard any tough stalks. It takes longer to cook than spinach or chard and is very high in nutritional value.

LETTUCE: It is best to select leaf varieties rather than the heading type. They are easier to grow and quicker to produce for eating. You can eat the thinnings in a few weeks or, if you do as I did one

25

year and accidently overplant, you can eat the delicate seedlings in salad in ten days. Keep thinning as the lettuce grows, and pick the outer leaves. If it is hot when your lettuce is in the seedling stage, cover the planter with window screening to diffuse the heat and light. When the plants begin to toughen and go to seed, continue to keep them moist and wait until they produce new leaves again in the early fall. Remember, lettuce likes cool weather, so you may have to move it occasionally when the sun is very hot.

BEANS: Both bush and pole beans will do well in a container garden with a good soil mixture and will give a good yield if watered well. Sow when the weather is warm and follow the directions for sowing on the package. Beans do well in pots. Tell your nursery clerk what you are doing and ask his advice on the best container. Pole beans will have to be staked.

SQUASH: All summer squashes are sure-fire crops for a beginning gardener. They grow rapidly and can be eaten when they are very young. In fact, they should be eaten young not only for taste, but because they will grow weighty and cumbersome for the container. Use a large, round, and deep container if you can, as squashes have a long root system, and sow according to the directions on the package. When they have grown into young plants, do not overwater or you will have more leaves than vegetables.

TOMATOES: Tomatoes are a joy to grow because they are so prolific, but they take longer to germinate, and must be sown when the weather is warm or indoors in peat pots for transplanting in warm weather. It is advisable to start with small plants until you are gardening with confidence. Most larger tomatoes will have to be staked and the plants tied to the stake with a soft cloth that won't cut into the stalks. Plant them securely, protect them from too much wind, direct heat, or cold nights, and give them plenty of water throughout their growth period.

Tomatoes generally produce later in the growing season because they have to be grown in warm weather. Do not be put off by the scraggly vines as they get older, especially if they give a good yield.

For your first gardening experience, it would be best to try a cherry tomato which grows anywhere and produces a sizable crop, or the pixie variety which yields a slightly larger tomato. Any tomato plant larger than a cherry variety needs room for roots—at least 1½ feet of soil. When transplanting, feed with fish emulsion (½ teaspoon to each ½ gallon of water). Repeat every five days for two weeks. Do not overwater, but keep moist. Start with a couple of small plants and posts, and you will be surprised. Remember, you can add to your container garden with the rooted plants from your country kitchen.

HERBS: I think a container garden is complete only with herbs, and if your space is very limited, they may be the only crop possible. For the beginning gardener, small plants bought in the nursery are advisable, although parsley, dill, and savory germinate quickly and grow especially well from seeds. Herbs should be snipped frequently to insure proper growth and a bushing effect.

Snip the tiny top leaves with your nail or small scissors. If you do this continually, your herbs will grow very thick. When the plants are young, be very careful not to break or injure the main stem or stalks of the nonbushy herbs like tarragon, dill, or basil. Snip off the leaves, not the stems, until they grow larger and produce many shoots. Bushy herbs like thyme or oregano have many stalks and cannot be injured easily, but you must be gentle with all young herbs. When the weather gets too cold you can bring the pots into the house and put them in a well-lighted place for the winter. If you do this, continue to feed and fertilize. When they get beyond your ability to utilize or begin to lose life or go to seed, they should be picked for drying and storing (see Chapter 3).

OTHER CROPS: You can even purchase dwarf fruit trees, some of which bear the first season if you get them when they are one or two years old. They can be covered and/or stored in the winter and brought out each spring. Check with a nursery or seed catalog. Other vegetables like cucumbers, green peppers, eggplant, and winter squashes are good ideas for your container garden, but for your first season, do not overextend the crop variety.

Sowing, Watering, and Thinning

SOWING: It is important not to overseed your planter, for an excess of seedlings makes the thinning process quite a chore. After you have sown according to the package directions, cover each container with plastic in which you have punched holes to allow air to circulate. I find it helpful to put a stake (a chopstick is good) in each planter to give a tentlike space for air circulation under the cover. The plastic cover acts as an incubator and greatly speeds up germinations, as well as protecting the seeds from browsing birds.

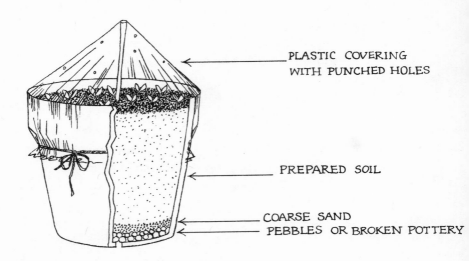

PLASTIC COVERING
WITH PUNCHED HOLES

PREPARED SOIL

COARSE SAND
PEBBLES OR BROKEN POTTERY

WATERING: Remove the plastic to water lightly. Use a fine spray attachment on the hose, or a watering can. You must water carefully to avoid routing and floating the seeds or damaging the delicate seedlings. Watering depends on the amount of sun on your garden and how quickly the soil dries out. The soil should be kept moist, but not soggy. When plants are 1½ to 2 inches high, remove the plastic: at first, roll it back during the day but keep the plants covered at night, then gradually remove it altogether.

THINNING: If you have a good soil you can be assured that the majority of seeds will germinate. Follow the directions on the package for sowing and thinning. When you begin the thinning process, use a pair of tiny pointed scissors. Clip off the seedlings at the soil line for nonroot vegetables, and pull out the excess root-vegetable seedlings with tweezers. Keep the thinnings to use in your salad of the day.

Predators

It is unlikely that in a container garden you will have much trouble with insects, and a healthy plant, like a healthy body, has good resistance to disease. Keeping the soil moist helps ward off insects. All strong-smelling flowers, like marigolds, and herbs and onions will act as insect repellents, and are good companions for your vegetables. If you do get a rash of unwanted bugs, consult the end of Chapter 8 for information on biological pest control.

A special dinner for mature plants can be made by placing a few days' vegetable parings, scraps, and egg shells in the blender and, with some water, blending into a liquid. Pour this into the soil around the plants every two weeks for extra nourishment.

Mulching for the Next Year

To prepare the soil for the next season when your crops have completed their yielding cycle, you can compost and mulch the soil for reuse. For a month or two after harvest, continue to pour the liquid dinner into the soil, turning under with a trowel, or in larger containers with a hand spade. Chop vegetable parings fine and turn these under too. If you have some fertilizer left over from the growing season, add it to the soil. Then cover all the containers with whatever mulch you have collected (oak leaves, lawn clippings from a park, or even hay), and let it decompose through the winter months. It will be fine to cultivate the following spring. Or, if you have had immense success with your summer crops, start investigating what you can grow throughout the winter.

29

To a great extent, the secrets for successful gardening are transmitted by word of mouth. This is why the collective or communal gardening concept is so healthy and productive. Although in this chapter you are referred to your nurseryman (or woman) for advice, don't hesitate to ask any good gardener for ideas and hints, especially anyone with a flourishing garden in your own area. Happy container gardening!

ADDITIONAL READING

Darlington, Jeanne. *Grow Your Own*. Berkeley, Ca.: The Bookworks.

Organic Gardening and Farming. Emmaus, Pa.: Rodale Press. (A good monthly magazine.)

Pendergast, Chuck. *Introduction to Organic Gardening*. Los Angeles: Nash Publishing Corporation.

Rodale, J.I., and staff. *The Encyclopedia of Organic Gardening*. Emmaus, Pa.: Rodale Press.

Schafer, Violet. *Herbcrafts*. San Francisco: Yerba Buena Press.

SEEDS

W. Atlee Burpee Company	*or*	Clinton, Iowa 52732
3124 Burpee Building	*or*	Riverside, Ca. 92502
Philadelphia, Pa. 19132		

CHAPTER 3

Preserving Fruits and Vegetables

ONE DAY recently, while I was in the kitchen stirring some plum jam on the stove, the mail woman brought a letter from my mother. She enclosed some very old recipes that she had brought from Wisconsin before she was married in North Dakota in 1933. One of them called for a "basket" of plums, and made me laugh. While I continued to stir, I read:

Dear Sharon:
Here are these old jelly and jam recipes. They are sort of vague, so you will have to convert them. For instance, the Plum and Muskmelon Conserve would have to be cut down considerably. Thirty or forty years ago, a basketful of plums meant a half a bushel or so. One uncooked jelly recipe I had said to set the glasses in the sun to jell. If you try this recipe for grape jelly, put one glass in the window and see what happens. It doesn't keep as long and you can't seal with paraffin on it. My mother used to make green or ripe tomato preserves often. The lemon is a must (sliced thin). She made the green tomatoes into preserves in the fall when frost came before the tomatoes ripened. If they were large and green, we would cut them from the vine (with a stem), wrap in newspaper and put them in the root cellar. They would ripen in the next few weeks. Or we would pull up vines of green tomatoes and hang them upside down in the root cellar. They would ripen that way also.

When you ask about things I often recall information that I hadn't thought of for years. For instance, Mother cooked meatballs or meat patties and put them in five-pound lard pails (they didn't need to be sealed) and poured melted fat over them. I don't know if it was lard (pork fat) or tallow (beef fat) or a mixture of both. We stored them in the root cellar because it was cool, but if we brought them upstairs and kept them at room temperature for a while, we could remove enough for a meal without disturbing the rest.

She canned rhubarb raw! Just sliced it and packed it in jars and put it under running water. (I remember the old pump was our running water and I helped with the pumping.) The secret was to fill all the air spaces in the rhubarb so we would check often to see if more air bubbles were coming to the top. When they quit bubbling (a few taps or gentle bumps would help too) they were sealed just like any canned fruit. Made good pie and jam in the winter time . . .

Love, *Mother*

Part of the letter goes back some fifty years, but even thirty years ago when I was a child in a small North Dakota plains town, my mother kept a huge garden and put up scores of jars of fruit, vegetables, and preserves for the winter. She says she would have been ashamed if her pantry had not been full by the late fall.

When we came to California at the beginning of the Second World War, both of my parents continued for many years to follow the customs and traditions of their farm upbringing. Mother canned, made preserves, baked bread, and kept chickens, even in the Southern California suburbs. Eventually the war changed the quality and availability of food in the country. My sister and I hated the job of coloring that wretched margarine we all had to use. Gradually, for one reason or another, like most of the midwestern immigrants, we succumbed to the changes of postwar affluence, and now Mother rarely cans, though she still makes jam when she gets a windfall of fruit. Dad has become the bread baker and is quite constant about the practice; I truly doubt that he will ever accept plastic bread. The chickens disappeared years ago because of zoning laws and the problems of caring for them. For a long time my parents drove to a small chicken ranch to buy fresh, fertile eggs, but the land developers swallowed up the small farmers in that area, and only in the last couple of years have fresh, fertile eggs been available again in their urban area.

So, they tried, but eventually gave up many of their habits—a familiar story in the last twenty-five years. Yet I can see my parents as pretty resourceful still and it is curious to see many of their friends from the city now moving to the country and reestablishing habits they were eased out of so many years ago.

Today, for the most part, preserving, canning, and freezing tend to be impractical for the city or suburban dweller. The "apartmentite" has a space problem, and market prices for fresh fruits and vegetables in bulk can be prohibitive for canning. But those who have access to small quantities of farm-fresh produce at a reasonable price will not regret the results of preserving and freezing, however small the amount. And a little preserving, if only for gifts, is worth the effort. But no matter how great or small a volume you preserve each year, it is necessary to become well acquainted with the preparational methods. Therefore, the following instructions constitute a reasonably complete guide to preserving fruits and vegetables.

CANNING

Most standard cookbooks contain complete instructions on canning. A large canning pan, which runs from five to seven dollars in hardware and houseware stores, usually has good directions and a timetable for canning both fruits and vegetables. It is important to know in the beginning that canning vegetables takes a much longer time (unless you use a pressure cooker) than fruits; and nonacid fruits and vegetables (all but tomatoes and pickled vegetables) *must* be properly cooked for they are subject to the Clostridium Botulinum bacteria (commonly known as botulism), which survives in an airless container. This bacteria can be fatal, so do not skimp on cooking time and discard any leaking jar or one that spurts air upon opening. DO NOT TASTE ANY SUSPICIOUS VEGETABLES. Fruit can

35

become moldy or discolored if it has not been properly sealed. Even though acid fruits are not subject to botulism, you should discard any jars that seem to contain spoiled food.

If you are using a standard canning pan for processing, you can place more jars in the pan the moment the previous batch is finished. This makes a continuous flow. With a pressure cooker or canner (the pressure canner is simply a large pressure cooker), the pressure is released slowly through the valve, so the jars must be kept in the cooker for ten minutes after it is finished.

The two common methods of canning are "cold pack," and "kettle" or "hot pack." Cold pack means to pack the raw fruit (vegetables are always cooked before they are put into jars) tightly into jars and pour boiling syrup or boiling water over the fruit to within an inch of the top of the jar. The lids are screwed on and the jars are set on a rack in a large kettle in hot, not boiling, water. The jars must not touch each other or they may break. The water is brought to a boil and the cooking time is gauged from the boiling moment. The water should be kept at a gentle boil the entire time. I think the best results are obtained when the water comes to the neck of the jar. Keep the lid tightly on the kettle while cooking. The heat sterilizes and seals the lids. You can also steam the jars above hot water and obtain the same results, but it is easier to maintain the necessary heat by letting the water circulate around the jars.

Hot-pack canning means cooking the fruit or vegetable first, packing it into jars, and covering with cooking liquid. The advantage of this method is that you do not waste space since the food won't shrink while in the canning pan. With cold pack you run the risk of shrinkage, but it is the only sensible way to handle soft fruit as cooking them first makes many fruits mushy; though my mother says that she usually canned with the hot-pack method to conserve jar space.

Types of Containers

I do not can in tins. Jars are readily available and easier to use, and

36

are more pleasing on the shelf. Here are the four types of jar lids for canning.

The clamp type (No. 4) is rare today unless you have a grandmother with a stash. It is most commonly seen in specialty shops where it is sold dearly as a decorator item.

PORCELAIN - LINED SCREW CAP   METAL SCREW CAP   SELF-SEALING CAP   CLAMP-TYPE LID

RUBBER RING   METAL SCREW BAND   METAL CAP   GLASS TOP   RUBBER RING

To use No. 1 and No. 2, screw the lids on tightly, then give a quarter turn back to allow steam to escape during processing. Use the same procedure for the clamp lids (No. 4), if you have them. The new "self-sealing" lids (No. 3), commonly sold in most markets, should be screwed on *tightly* before processing. Then boiling water is poured over the lid.

Simple Canning Steps for Both Fruits and Vegetables

1. Check all jars for nicks and cracks. Use new rubber seals for jar lids 1, 2, and 4, and new lids for 3.

2. Wash and scald jars and lids.

3. Select and wash firm, ripe produce. Then prepare according to the chart on pages 39–42.

4. Pack fruit or vegetables into jars, leaving proper head space of:
   1 inch for starchy foods (corn, peas, beans)
   ½ inch for fruits and other vegetables.

5. Add liquid as called for in whichever recipe you are using. Release bubbles by running a knife around the inside of the jar.

6. Wipe the neck of the jar completely clean and put on scalded lids. Remember to give a quarter turn back to rubber ring jars and to pour boiling water over self-seal lids.

7. Process jars in hot water bath, steam, or pressure cooker. Follow recipes and instructions carefully.

8. Remove after the required amount of time and set on wood or folded towels.

9. Immediately tighten rubber ring jars and let cool for 12 hours.

10. After 12 hours, you can remove rings from self-sealing jars and test the seal by pressing the cap. If it stays down, the seal is good. Store jars.

Special Canning Hints

1. Pierce unpeeled fruit to prevent the skin from bursting.

2. Remove skin by blanching or scalding in boiling water for a minute or so until the skin comes off easily.

3. If possible, pack halved fruit center-side down to prevent syrup from filling center cavity, thereby insuring tighter packing.

4. Do not put freshly canned jars that are still hot in a draft or on cold metal counters.

5. Add sliced lemon to jars of pears, and cinnamon sticks to apricots and peaches.

6. It is easiest to kettle can and treat small amounts of berries and cherries as in making jam. (See jam making.)

7. For flavor, add two or three pits to the jar when canning apricots.

Remember the possible danger in canning nonacid vegetables. Nowadays freezing is actually a safer and tastier method of preserving these vegetables.

Vegetable Preparation Guide
As a general rule, add 1 teaspoon of salt to each quart of vegetables.

	Hot Water Processing Time	Pressure Cooker Processing Time
Asparagus: Wash, cook 5 minutes in boiling water, pack hot and cover with hot cooking water.	3 hrs.	30 min. / 10 lbs.
Beans (Green, string, snap, wax): Wash, cut off ends and strings, cut in 1-inch pieces, cook 5 minutes in boiling water, pack hot and cover with hot cooking water.	3 hrs.	25 min. / 10 lbs.
Beans (Lima, pinto, soy, etc.): Shell, grade if desired, cook in boiling water 10 minutes, pack hot and cover with hot cooking water.	3 hrs.	50 min. / 10 lbs.
Beets: Wash, retain 1-inch stem, cook 15 minutes, or until skin slips, slip off skins, pack hot whole or sliced and cover with hot cooking water.	3 hrs.	35 min. / 10 lbs.
Carrots: Wash, scrape, leave whole or slice as desired, cook in boiling water 10 minutes, pack hot and cover with hot cooking water.	2 hrs.	30 min. / 10 lbs.
Corn: Remove husks, cut kernels from cob, cook 5 minutes in boiling water, pack hot and cover with hot cooking water.	3 hrs.	85 min. / 10 lbs.

	Hot Water Processing Time	Pressure Cooker Processing Time
Greens (All types): Wash, remove tough stems, boil in small amount of water 15 minutes, pack hot and cover with hot cooking water.	2 hrs.	90 min. / 10 lbs.
Parsnips: Wash, cook 15 minutes in boiling water, cut in ½-inch cubes or slice thinly, pack hot and cover with hot cooking water.	2 hrs.	40 min. / 10 lbs.
Peas: Shell and wash, cook 5 minutes in boiling water, pack hot and cover with hot cooking water.	3 hrs.	40 min. / 10 lbs.
Potatoes: Wash, peel cut in 1-inch cubes, cook in boiling water 2 minutes, drain, pack hot and cover with hot cooking water.	3 hrs.	40 min. / 10 lbs.
Squash (All types): Wash, peel winter squash, cook in boiling water until tender, pack hot and cover with hot cooking water.	3 hrs.	90 min. / 10 lbs.
Sweet Potatoes and Yams: Wash, cook in boiling water until skins slip, peel, cut in 2-inch cubes, pack hot and cover with medium or thick syrup, boiling hot.	3 hrs.	90 min. / 10 lbs.
Tomatoes (All types): Wash, blanch, and cover with hot water or cook 1 minute in boiling water and pack hot, covering with hot cooking water.	Cold pack: 45 min. Hot pack: 5 min.	10 min. / 5 lbs.
Turnips (Rutabaga, white): Process as parsnips.		

Few readers will can all of these vegetables, but for all of us there is a historical experience in understanding the process.

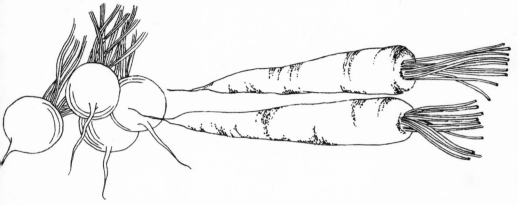

Fruit Preparation Guide

Fruit can be packed in syrup, in fruit juice, or in clear water for those who prefer the natural taste. When you use syrup, prepare it in advance and pour boiling hot over the fruit:

Syrup	Honey or Sugar		Water
Thin	½	1	3 parts
Medium	½	1	2 parts
Thick	½	1	1 part

Honey is not necessarily recommended for syrup because of its prohibitive cost today.

	Pt. & Qt. Glass Jars	Syrup
Apples: Steam or boil to wilt, pack in hot syrup or water.	15 min.	Thin
Same as above but dry pack.	20 min.	
Bake or boil whole, pack in hot syrup.	5 min.	
Applesauce, pack hot.	10 min.	

41

	Pt. & Qt. Glass Jars	Syrup
Apricots: Halved and pitted, pack raw.	25 min.	Medium
Precook 5 minutes and pack hot.	15 min.	
Blackberries: Pack raw, cover with hot syrup.	20 min.	Medium
Blueberries, Dewberries, Huckleberries, Loganberries, Blackberries, and Raspberries: Precook 10 minutes and pack hot.	5 min.	
Cherries: Stem, do not pit, pack raw, cover with hot syrup.	25 min.	Sweet, Medium Sour, Thick
Peaches: Halved and pitted, pack raw, cover with hot syrup.	Firm, 35 min. Soft, 25 min.	Medium
Precook 5 minutes and pack hot.	15 min.	
Pears: Halved and cored, pack raw, cover with hot syrup.		Medium
Precook 5 minutes and pack hot.	20 min.	
Pineapples: Slice, core, and skin, pack raw, cover with hot syrup.	30 min.	Thin
Plums: Do not pit or peel, pack raw, cover with hot syrup.	20 min.	Medium
Precook 5 minutes and pack hot.	5 min.	
Rhubarb: Precook until tender and pack hot.	5 min.	Thick
Strawberries: Pack raw.	45 min.	Medium
Precook until tender and pack hot.	5 min.	

FREEZING FRUITS AND VEGETABLES

Freezing fruits and vegetables is little trouble if you follow some simple steps:

1. Select firm, ripe produce. Cut away any bad spots.

2. Try to do the preparation in the early morning or in the cool evening directly after the produce has been picked or purchased.

3. Fruits and vegetables should be clean and packed very tightly to prevent air pockets.

4. Allow 1 inch of head space for expansion, use freezing containers of plastic or jars sold for freezing, and follow the instructions on the box.

VEGETABLES

1. Use only fresh vegetables.

2. Scald or blanch in boiling water first to stop the fermentation action that causes color and flavor changes. You do not need a blancher; simply use a large pan and a metal colander or wire basket for dipping the vegetables. Time the scalding carefully from the moment the water returns to a boil. Use 8 times the amount of water to the amount of vegetable.

3. Immediately after scalding, plunge the vegetables into ice water, or hold under cold running water.

4. Drain and pack well in plastic cartons or freezer bags. Leave 1 inch or 1½ inches of head space for expansion. Otherwise eliminate as much air as possible.

5. Sharp freeze. When ready to use, cook from the frozen stage as you would commercially frozen vegetables. If you wish to use frozen vegetables in salad, simply dip vegetables in boiling water until thawed.

6. Do not salt vegetables until serving.

Vegetable Preparation Guide

Asparagus: Wash well and break at the tender point. Scald 1 to 2 minutes, depending on thickness of spear. Chill for 3 times the scalding time.

Beans (Green or wax): Select young tender beans. Cut off stem and blossom end. Scald yellow wax beans ½ minute longer. Scald French-cut beans (cut diagonally in thin slices) about 1 minute.

43

Scald whole green beans for 5 minutes. Chill 3 times the length of scalding time.

Beets: Cut off tops, leaving a bit of the top on as a finger hold. (See "Spinach and Other Greens" for freezing beet tops.) Cook in very little water until the skins slip. Spread on a tray to cool. Peel and slice, or pack baby beets whole.

Broccoli: Trim stalks to the tender portion, and cut these into uniform pieces. Cut spears the length of the container. Scald separately for 3 to 5 minutes, depending on thickness. Chill rapidly in ice water.

Brussels Sprouts: Sort according to size, and wash well to remove bugs. Scald from 3 to 4 minutes, depending on size. Chill in ice water 3 times as long as the scalding time.

Cauliflower: Trim into flowerlets. Wash well or let stand in light brine of salt water for 10 minutes. Scald for 3½ to 4½ minutes, depending on size. Chill immediately in ice water.

Corn on the Cob: Use young, juicy corn ears. Husk and remove all the silk. Scald by dropping a few ears into rapidly boiling water for 5 minutes. Chill immediately for 3 times the scalding time to make sure the cob is well cooled. Do not wrap more than two ears together. To cook: Drop ears into a large quantity of cold water and bring the water slowly to a boil in order to thaw out the cob without overcooking the kernels. Boil for not more than 2 minutes as corn overcooks rapidly. Or, if you have frozen corn in foil, turn back the foil and brush with butter, re-cover and roast in a moderate oven for 20 to 25 minutes.

Corn (Whole kernels): Scald corn on the cob for 2 to 3 minutes. Chill immediately in ice water or running cold water. Cut corn from the cob without cutting cob. Pack dry and freeze quickly.

Peas: Use only very young peas. Shell and scald from 1 to 3 minutes, depending on size of pea. Chill immediately and dry well before freezing.

Peppers: Use sweet peppers. Remove stem and seeds. Cut into small pieces and freeze directly. If you wish to freeze whole stuffed

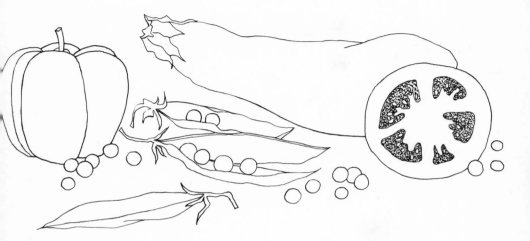

peppers, scald seeded peppers for 3 to 5 minutes. Chill in running water or ice water, drain and stuff with cooked filling. Freeze for not more than 4 months.

Spinach and Other Greens: Wash well in lukewarm water. Scald or steam only long enough to wilt the green so it will pack easily. Quickly chill in ice water or in the refrigerator if steamed. Leave room in container for expansion.

Summer Squashes: Select very young squash with tender skins. Wash and trim blossom and stem ends. Cut into ½-inch pieces and scald for 1 minute, or steam for 2 minutes. Chill quickly in ice water.

Tomatoes: These do not freeze well as their natural texture will not preserve. I recommend canning if you come into a good supply of tomatoes. Otherwise, make soup and freeze it, or make relishes and tomato paste. If you do have freezer room, you can freeze tomatoes whole without peeling, slicing, or coring by just washing and placing them uncovered in the freezer. To use, run under cold water to slip the skins. They will be good for cooking, but too mushy for salads.

45

FRUIT

1. For fruit that discolors easily, prepare no more than 5 cups at a time.

2. A sharp freeze is best for most fruit, providing the fruit is reasonably cool to begin with.

3. When ready to use, thaw slowly, starting in the refrigerator.

Fruit Preparation Guide

Apples: Apples will turn dark if they are the least bit green and are not treated with lemon syrup or powdered ascorbic or citric acid (available from druggists). Peel if not organically grown, core, slice, and pack tightly as other fruit.

Apricots: Pit and halve apricots for freezing. You may use a light syrup made of lemon juice and sugar or honey and water. Or sprinkle lemon juice over the apricots. Either will preserve the color.

Berries: Berries should not be mushy, and should be well cleaned and free from stems and leaves. Strawberries should be sugared, but sweetening is not necessary for other berries. Crumple wax paper to fill in the top in order to exclude more air from the container.

Oranges: Peel, section or slice, and sugar slightly, and pack as directed for other fruit.

Peaches and Pears: Blanch to remove skin. Pit or core, and prepare and pack as for apricots.

Plums: Plums do not need sugar for freezing, but it is wise to steam them slightly to keep their skins from getting tough.

DRYING VEGETABLES AND HERBS

No directions are included in this section for drying fruits because, to my taste, dried fruits need sulphuring to preserve the color and vitamin content. Sun-dried fruit also requires attention to ward off insects, and both processes take more space than city or suburban dwellers can usually afford. Although the prices are high, dried fruits are available throughout the country.

Drying vegetables, however, is fun, historic, decorative, and useful. Try stringing and hanging beans and peppers for an especially attractive addition to the country kitchen. Perhaps you have heard of the phrase "leather britches," which is the down-South name for dried beans that have been strung.

VEGETABLES

Beans (String, green, snap, wax):   Wash, dry well, and string on a heavy thread, tying each bean separately. Beans will wrinkle and dry in time. Hang for several months and when you are ready to

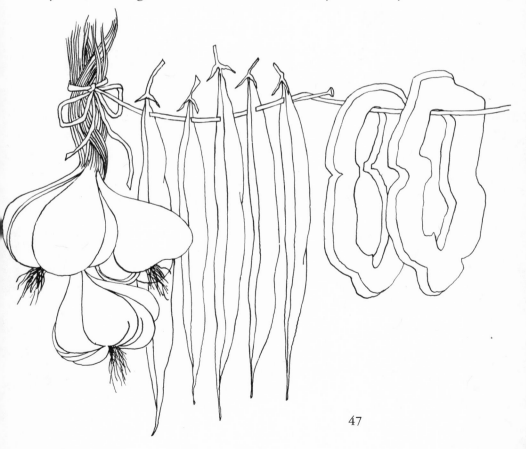

47

use them, remove the string, wash, and put on to cook. After they boil once, pour off the water to prevent any bitterness, and cook or steam until tender. It is nice to add onions and a ham bone for more flavor.

Garlic: Garlic fresh from the field or garden should be laid in the sun to dry. Do not remove stem or fine roots. When the bulbs have turned white, braid together, adding new stems and bulbs as you go, making a long braid of closely woven bulbs backed by a heavy interlace of stems. Wrap end of stems with colorful fabric and hang in the kitchen.

Onions and Leeks: Peel and slice in thin rings. String to dry. Soak and drain like peppers before using. This is a nice thing to do if someone gives you a supply of home-grown onions.

Peppers (All types):   Small red peppers may be dried whole. All others should be cut in rings and strung in the same manner as beans. All peppers will become very dark in drying. Soak and drain before using in cooking.

Shelled Beans and Peas: Shell, sort, and spread on trays or drying frames. Stir daily until completely dry. Store in covered jars.

Herbs

Pick herbs while they are flowering and before they go to seed. Wash lightly and shake to drain. You can spread them to dry on a tray in a warm place out of the sun to protect the color, or tie in little bunches and hang upside down in your kitchen. When they are completely dry, store stem and all in tightly covered jars to preserve flavor. They look beautiful on the kitchen shelf and you can extract a piece and crumble it between your fingers to use whenever desired.

JAMS, JELLIES, AND CONSERVES

The most rewarding sight in preserving food, to my taste, is a shelf or two full of my own jams, jellies, and conserves. Nearly everyone likes a little jam or jelly once in a while, and it is gratifying to be able to offer the unmistakable taste of homemade fruit spreads.

They make beautiful gifts for special occasions or just to take when you visit a friend. I have vivid memories of my mother making jam in the red brick house where we lived in Southern California. We had an old apricot tree which gave a handsome yield each year. I remember the dish full of the skimmings from the top of the jam which we ate on bread.

Of the several methods of making jam, the most common is to cook it on the top of the stove with fruit pectin. Pectin is the substance that makes it jell. Or there are uncooked jams made to be kept in the refrigerator until eaten. There are sunbaked jams and there is also an old-fashioned slow-cook method which does not need pectin. For the latter, simply mash the fruit, add an equal amount of sugar and spread in a shallow pan. Then bake it in a low oven (250–275°) until thick (about 5 hours). Seal according to the jar manufacturer's directions and store.

For best results I suggest following the clear directions on the pectin packages for good jams and jelly, both cooked and uncooked. I prefer to use a cup or so less sugar than directed as I do not like preserves too sweet. Other than that, I follow the directions carefully to insure the thickening of the jam. Be certain to select a pectin that has a fruit pectin source and no additional chemicals to aid thickening. Pectin is found in most fruits to some degree, and the most common and reliable source is apples. The following group of recipes includes one for making and preserving pectin.

The recipes given here are favorites that have been passed on by my family and friends. Since I find a great deal of confusion over the names of these spreads, I offer my categories:

Jam—an unstrained fruit spread;

Jelly—a strained fruit spread;

Marmalade—a spread made from citrus fruits including the juice and rind;

Conserve—a sweet, jamlike relish often containing nuts which is usually made of several ingredients and is delicious served with meat or fowl;

Relish—a sweet or sour spread or accompaniment generally made from several vegetables;

Chutney—a hot relish of East Indian origin made from fruits and spices; and

Preserves—any food that is preserved or canned in jars or cans for later use. We commonly refer to the process of preserving fruit as canning, and the word preserves is often used to refer to jams and jellies only.

Hints for Making Jams, Jellies, and Conserves

1. Add lemon juice to your recipe, especially if you do not have quite enough fruit. The juice adds flavor and the acid assists the jell.

2. Honey may be used in place of sugar, although, again, honey is expensive. Use half as much honey and cook 1 to 2 minutes longer to thicken. Honey tends not to create as thick a spread, so when using it with fruits low in pectin (berries, pears, peaches, and cherries), add extra pectin.

3. The self-sealing lids are perfect for jams and jellies. Simply follow the directions in the boxes. But, if you want to make use of old jars and therefore must use paraffin, follow my mother's pouring method for the best protection for your preserves:

Fill jars of jam or jelly quite full, at least to the grooves of the lid. Carefully pour (very slowly if the jam is hot) a thin layer of paraffin. Let this set for a day or so as paraffin tends to pull away from the sides as it cools. Then pour over another layer of hot paraffin and tilt the jar so it reaches the sides and covers the area which may be exposed from the first layer. Fill the last layer of paraffin to the top of the jar.

Homemade Pectin

Fully ripened apples make a clear pectin, but the early small green apples thicken best.

Approximate yield: 1 quart pectin from 1 pound of apples

1. Wash and core apples. Cut in thin slices.

2. Add 1 pint of water per pound of apples, and boil slowly in a covered pot for 15 minutes.

3. Strain free-flowing juice through light muslin or cheesecloth.

4. Return the pulp to the pot and add the same amount of water. Cook slowly for another 15 minutes. Strain out all juice through a cloth again, this time squeezing the pulp dry.

5. Combine the two juices and use immediately or bring to a full boil and pour into sterilized jars and seal like jam for later use. Use 1 cup of this pectin to 6 cups of prepared fruit in your jam and jelly recipes.

Uncooked Grape Jelly

1. Put 1 quart of grapes and 14 cups of water in a saucepan.

2. Simmer until fruit is soft. Then place a thin cloth in a colander and mash fruit so that juice is collected in a pan under the colander.

3. Measure in sugar, ½ cup to 1 cup of juice.

4. Beat 10 minutes with a spoon and pour into sterilized glasses.

5. Cover and store in the refrigerator. This jells in 3 to 4 days.

This is my mother's recipe—very midwestern.

Old-Fashioned Green Tomato Preserves

> 2 quarts small green tomatoes
> 3 cups sugar
> ¼ sliced lemon
> ½ teaspoon dry ginger
> ½ teaspoon cinnamon

Peel tomatoes, leaving the stem ends, if possible. Pour boiling water (to cover) over tomatoes, let come to a boil, and drain. Sprinkle tomatoes with sugar, let stand, add lemon and spices. Boil gently until they are translucent. Pour into shallow pans and allow to stand overnight. Pack tomatoes cold into sterilized jars. Reheat syrup, strain, pour over tomatoes in jar and seal.

51

The three recipes that follow are especially nice for those who have fruit trees that get overloaded with fruit at one time.

Apple Butter

1. Wash, core, and cut apples into small pieces.
2. Put into a pot with a little water (very little—only enough to prevent burning) and cook over a low heat until softened.
3. Put through a sieve or wire strainer.
4. To each 4 cups of apple pulp add: 2 cups sugar, 1 teaspoon cinnamon, and ½ teaspoon each allspice and cloves.
5. Cook slowly until thick enough (several hours), either on top of the stove or in a shallow pan in a slow oven, 250°.
6. Do not add spices until the fruit is thick and you are ready to pour it into sterilized jars for sealing.

Fig Jam

Personally, I don't like the taste of figs in any form, but for those who do and especially for those who have a tree, jam is a good item to make from this fruit, which should be used as soon as it is ripe.

> 6 cups chopped white or black figs
> 4½ cups sugar
> 6 tablespoons lemon juice

Peel and chop figs, add sugar and lemon juice. Boil rapidly until thickened, about 25 minutes. Remove scum, pour into sterilized jars and seal.

Persimmons I love. They are a beautiful and delicate fruit. They can be eaten ripe with lemon, or frozen ripe and served without thawing as a sherbetlike dessert (cut in half and scoop out the pulp). The secret is to eat them very ripe. Pick them hard and set in a sunny window until they are *very* soft.

Persimmon Butter

>4 cups persimmon pulp
>2 cups sugar
>cinnamon and cloves to taste

Use fully ripened persimmons. Scrape out pulp and measure. Add sugar and spice lightly with cinnamon and cloves. Boil, stirring frequently, until mixture is thickened and clear. Remove scum and pour into hot, sterilized jars and seal immediately.

Fresh Berry Jam (A lovely, healthful recipe)

>fresh raspberries or strawberries
>1 package pectin
>honey to taste

Mash berries, then place in blender with honey. Add pectin and blend briskly for about 2 minutes. Make small batches and pour into sterilized jars and store in the refrigerator.

For those who like fruit syrups on their waffles, hot cakes, French toast, or ice cream, here is a simple, delicious recipe which can be used for all fruits. Syrups make special holiday gifts too.

Fruit Syrup

1. Wash fruit well, core or pit, and peel fruit with thick or toughened skins.
2. Put a small amount in the blender and purée. Repeat.
3. Force pulp through a wire strainer.
4. To every 4 cups of fruit purée add:
>   1 cup water
>   3 tablespoons lemon juice
>   3 cups sugar or 1 ½ to 2 cups honey (decrease if
>   desired)
5. Bring all ingredients to a boil and cook for 5 minutes, stirring constantly.
6. Remove from heat, skim off the foam, and pour into sterile jars and seal.

Max's Mother's Cranberry Sauce (She served this with any meat or fowl)

>   1 package fresh or frozen cranberries
>   2 cups water
>   1 cup sugar
>   1 cinnamon stick broken into pieces
>   ½ each lemon and orange sliced very thin

Simmer lemon, orange, and cinnamon pieces in water for 4 to 5 minutes. Add cranberries and sugar, and simmer until cranberries are tender, about 5 more minutes. Do not overcook. Pour into sterilized jars and store in the refrigerator.

Here is the recipe which called for a "basket" of plums.

Plum and Muskmelon (Cantaloupe) Conserve

> 6 cups pitted and mashed plums
> ½ large cantaloupe
> 3 tablespoons lemon juice (about 1 lemon)
> 1 cup chopped walnuts
> 2 cups sugar
> 1 package pectin

Cook plums, lemon juice, and sugar with a tiny bit of water (only enough to prevent scorching). Cut melon in small pieces and add after plums have cooked about 7 to 8 minutes. Cook to a full boil and then remove and add nuts. Pour into sterilized jars and seal.

Rhubarb is really a vegetable, but because it is always sweetened in cooking, we regard it as a fruit. Don't eat the leaves as they contain a toxic element.

Rhubarb Conserve

> 4 cups rhubarb
> 1 cup raisins
> 1 tablespoon grated orange rind
> ¼ cup orange juice
> 3 cups sugar
> ½ cup nut meats

Wash and dice rhubarb. Add all other ingredients except nuts and cook, stirring occasionally, until thick and clear. Add nuts and pour into hot, sterilized jars and seal immediately.

Here's a fine one if you like peeling grapes!

Grape Conserve

>   1 pound slipskin-type grapes
>   1¼ cups sugar
>   ¼ small orange, ground or thinly sliced
>   ¼ teaspoon salt
>   ¼ cup chopped nuts
>   ¼ cup seedless raisins (optional)

Wash, drain, and remove grapes from stems. Scald and slip off skins and keep separate from the pulp. Cook pulp 10 minutes, or until seeds show. Press through sieve to remove seeds. To pulp add sugar, raisins, orange, and salt. Cook rapidly until mixture begins to thicken, stirring throughout. Add grape skins and cook for 10 minutes or until thick. Add chopped nuts and pour at once into sterilized jars and seal.

Making sweet/sour and hot relishes is another kitchen pleasure, especially since they can be made in small quantities. Relishes, a good accompaniment to meat and fowl, are nice holiday gifts. I like tart and hot relishes with cottage cheese or on cheese sandwiches. Chutnies are the relishes we associate with East Indian curry dishes, and they can vary from mild to hot. For those who like very hot relishes, I recommend additional cayenne pepper before serving.

Peach Chutney

>   4 quarts chopped peaches
>   5 cups vinegar
>   ½ cup chopped onion
>   ½ cup sugar
>   1 cup raisins
>   1 small garlic bulb

1 cup white mustard seed

1 ounce scraped ginger root, or 1 tablespoon powdered
ginger

½ teaspoon cayenne pepper

Peel peaches, remove pits, and chop coarsely. Add 2 cups of the
vinegar to peaches and cook until soft. Add 1 more cup of vinegar,
onion, sugar, raisins, mustard seed, ginger root, cayenne, and garlic.
Mix well and add remaining 2 cups of vinegar. Boil for 15 minutes,
pack in sterilized jars and seal.

English Chutney Sauce

1 dozen ripe tomatoes

1 pound apples, cored

¾ pound raisins

2 seeded sweet red peppers

6 small onions

¼ cup mint leaves

¼ cup white mustard seed

¼ cup salt

2 cups granulated sugar

1 quart vinegar

Chop tomatoes. Put other vegetables and mint leaves through the
food chopper or meat grinder. Place all ingredients in preserving
kettle, bring to boil. Cook slowly until thick and clear and pour into
sterile jars and seal.

Purple Plum Chutney

5 pounds fresh purple plums (about 8 cups prepared)

2 cups light brown sugar, firmly packed

2 cups white sugar

1½ cups cider vinegar

3 teaspoons crushed dried red peppers

57

> 4 teaspoons salt
> 4 teaspoons mustard seed
> 4 fat cloves garlic
> 1½ cups sweet Spanish onions, sliced on bias
> 1 cup preserved ginger, cut in thin slices
> 2 cups seedless raisins

Pit, seed, and halve plums. Set aside. Mix sugars and vinegar and bring to a boil. Add crushed chilies, salt, mustard seed, garlic, onion, ginger, and raisins. Mix well. Stir in plums. Bring to a boil, reduce heat, and simmer, uncovered, stirring frequently about 50 minutes or until thickened. Test by placing small amount of chutney on a saucer, chill in refrigerator; if it "sets up" (jells) the chutney is done. Pour into sterile jars and seal.

Quick Corn Relish

This compares favorably with corn relishes requiring a much longer preparation time.

> 1 cup vinegar
> ½ cup sugar
> 1 teaspoon salt
> ½ teaspoon Tabasco sauce
> ½ teaspoon mustard seed
> 1 teaspoon celery seed
> 2 1-pound cans whole kernel corn, drained, or an equivalent amount of frozen or fresh, cooked and cooled
> ¼ cup minced green pepper
> ¼ cup minced onion
> 2 pimientos, chopped

Combine vinegar, sugar, salt, Tabasco, mustard seed, and celery seed. Bring to a boil and cook 3 minutes. Add vegetables and heat until very hot, but not boiling. Cool in refrigerator, keeping covered, for 24 hours before serving.

Uncooked Garden Relish

> 1 small cabbage
> 4 medium onions, peeled
> 4 large carrots
> 2 medium sweet red peppers, seeded
> 2 medium green peppers, seeded
> ¼ cup salt
> 2 cups vinegar
> 2 cups sugar
> 1 tablespoon mustard seed
> 2 tablespoons celery seed

Chop vegetables fine or put through food grinder. Stir in salt and let stand about 3 hours. Drain, then rinse with fresh water and drain again, pressing the vegetables with your hand to squeeze out excess water. Combine vinegar, sugar, and spices and mix gently but thoroughly with the vegetables. Fill sterile jars and cover tightly. This relish keeps quite a while without sealing, but because the ingredients are nonacid, I strongly recommend sealing or storing in the refrigerator.

Tomato Relish

> 2 quarts ripe tomatoes
> 1 cup chopped celery
> 1 cup chopped white onions
> 2 cups diced tart apples
> 2 red peppers, chopped
> 12 green peppers, seeded and chopped
> 1½ cups vinegar
> 2¾ cups sugar
> 1 tablespoon salt
> 1 tablespoon broken cinnamon sticks
> ½ tablespoon whole cloves

2 tablespoons white mustard seed

Scald, peel, and chop tomatoes. Add other ingredients. Boil, stirring occasionally, until mixture is thickened. Pour into sterile jars and seal.

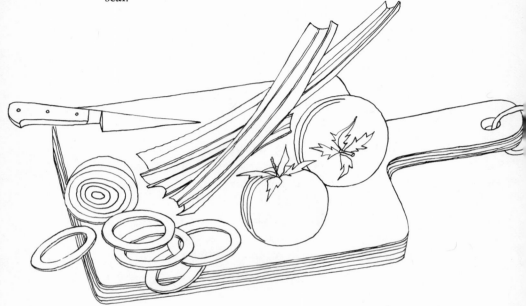

If you get a flood of tomatoes and get tired of canning or making relish, here is a recipe that you can always use:

Tomato Paste

> 4 quarts tomatoes
> 1 to 4 buds garlic
> 1 teaspoon cayenne pepper
> 2 sweet seeded red peppers
> salt to taste
> 2 tablespoons oil (optional)

Wash ripe tomatoes and slice without peeling. Add other

ingredients except oil and cook until soft. Put through a coarse sieve. Boil the pulp, stirring frequently, until it is the consistency of thick catsup. Place in the top of a double boiler and cook over hot water until it reaches the thickness of paste. Add oil and pack in sterile jars and seal. Half-pint jars are best.

Another favorite preserving experience is pickling. I have friends with a marvelous cucumber patch and they put up dozens of jars, many as gifts for their friends, every year. Every time I see a pickle, I think of their kitchen.

Dill Pickles

> 6 medium cucumbers
> ice water
> 1 medium onion, peeled and thinly sliced
> 6 dill sprigs
> 2 cups vinegar
> 1 cup water
> 1 cup sugar
> ⅓ cup salt

Cover cucumbers with ice water and let stand 4 hours. Drain. Do not peel cucumbers; simply cut them lengthwise to fit in pint jars. Pack in sterile jars, tucking in onion slices and dill. Combine vinegar, water, sugar, and salt. Bring to a boil and pour over cucumbers. Seal. Let stand a month before using.

Zucchini Pickles

These look and taste like fine bread-and-butter pickles.

> 2 quarts thinly sliced, unpeeled small zucchini squash
> 2 medium onions, peeled and thinly sliced
> ¼ cup salt

61

> 2 cups vinegar
> 2 cups sugar
> 1 teaspoon celery seed
> 2 teaspoons mustard seed
> 1 teaspoon turmeric
> ½ teaspoon dry mustard

Combine zucchini and onions, sprinkle with salt, and cover with cold water. Let stand 2 hours, drain, rinse with fresh water, then drain again. Combine remaining ingredients in a good-sized pot and bring to boiling. Cook 2 minutes. Add vegetables, remove from heat, and let stand 2 hours. Bring again to boiling and cook 5 minutes. Seal in sterile jars.

Pickled Carrot Sticks

> 1 pound carrots
> ¾ cup vinegar
> ¾ cup water
> ½ cup sugar
> 1 teaspoon mixed pickling spices

Slice the carrots in thin sticks, cover with boiling salted water, and cook 10 minutes. Drain. Combine vinegar, water, sugar, and spices in a large saucepan. Bring to a boil over moderate heat, then reduce heat and simmer 3 minutes. Pack carrot sticks in sterile jars and cover with the hot liquid. Seal.

For those who miss the old European delicatessen sauerkraut or for those who have never tasted a homemade variety, here is an easy small-batch recipe. You will need a wide-mouth gallon container, a plate slightly smaller than the inner diameter of the container, and a few large stones. Make as much as you want. The method is what's important.

Sauerkraut

1. Shred a head of cabbage and place at the bottom of the container.

2. Pulverize (use a mortar and pestle or a similar makeshift arrangement) ½ teaspoon each of dill, caraway, and celery seed. Mix with 1 teaspoon ground sea kelp (found in health food stores). Sprinkle this mixture over the cabbage.

3. Cover with cold water—approximately 2 quarts.

4. Place the plate over the cabbage and press it down carefully so it is submerged in the water and weight it down with a clean stone.

5. Cover and place in a warm room to begin fermentation.

These directions apply to one head of cabbage. Add spices and water in the same amount for each head of cabbage. Layer it and place the plate and stones over the final layer. If you are making a full crock, stop several inches below the top so it does not overflow during fermentation.

The time needed for fermentation varies according to the room temperature, anywhere from 7 to 10 days. You will need to scrape the scum as it ferments, so taste it after a week. It may be ready. Strain off the liquid and salt to taste. Since salt is not used in the fermentation, it will need salt for most people's taste. The method is of course fine for those who watch their salt intake. You can also add onions and other root vegetables to this fermentation process.

Herb Vinegars

Making vinegar is as much fun as making wine, and it is a super gift item. You can buy good apple cider or wine vinegar and add experimental combinations of fresh herbs, let set for a couple weeks inside in a sunny spot, taste, and if sufficiently spiced, strain, bottle, and cork or cap for later use.

Or, you can buy some sweet natural cider and let it stand,

uncovered, in a warm room for several weeks and it will turn to vinegar.

Or, if you are really energetic, you can make your own in the old-fashioned tradition.

Old-Fashioned Vinegar

1. Select a fruit to combine with tart apples. Pears are nice. You can use Concord grapes by themselves and they will make a splendid vinegar different from either cider or wine vinegar.

2. Clean and mash the fruit. For apples and pears, you will need a grinder (or a deep pot and a heavy stick like a baseball bat can be substituted). When making a lot of vinegar, mash with a two-by-four. I suggest performing this act outside, preferably with an audience.

3. Put the mashed fruit in a glass container or earthenware crock. Don't ferment things in metal. Cover with a cloth and tie with a string to keep away fruit flies. Leave a lot of head room for expansion in fermentation, about 20 to 25%.

4. Store in a garage or a basement if you have one. If not, a closet or pantry will have to do. Keep an eye on the fermentation and stir and taste the working mixture occasionally. It will take several months, possibly six.

5. When you like the flavor, strain and store in glass in a cool, dark place. Don't fasten lids too tightly and it will last for several years.

If the vinegar is too strong, dilute it with water. If it is too weak, add some good commercial vinegar. It's best not to use it for pickling preserves in the event the acidity is not right, although you can try it if you aren't worried about a failure. Try any herb combination for variety and make up your Christmas vinegar bottles. Here are a couple of suggestions.

Spice Vinegar (for cold vegetables, marinades, and basting)

> 1 quart cider vinegar
> 1 tablespoon whole allspice
> 1 tablespoon whole white pepper
> 1 tablespoon whole cloves
> 1 tablespoon whole coriander seed
> 1 teaspoon celery seed
> 2 tablespoons sugar
> 1 teaspoon salt
> small piece ginger root

Simmer vinegar and spices (except ginger root). Cool, pour into quart jar, and add ginger. Cover tightly and let stand for 10 days to 2 weeks. Strain with cloth and colander and vinegar is ready to use.

Garlic or Shallot Vinegar

This is a good mono-flavored vinegar for a tossed green salad or meat marinade.

> 1 quart vinegar
> 2 dozen shallots or 4 cloves garlic

Peel and chop shallots or garlic. Let stand in vinegar for 2 to 3 weeks. Strain and use.

Don't feel you must do everything in this chapter. You won't have time to bring in the mail or deliver the gifts you have made.

CHAPTER 4

Making
Beverages at Home

"Have some wine," the March Hare said in an engaging tone.

Alice looked around the table, but there was nothing on it but

tea. "I don't see any wine," she remarked.

"There isn't any," said the March Hare.

LEWIS CARROLL, *Alice in Wonderland*

THIS CHAPTER is devoted to the fun and art of making beer and fruit wines. All instructions have been simplified and scaled down in volume to make it possible for those with small work areas to produce a good supply of these beverages for their larders. There is an initial investment for the necessary supplies, but you will find these homemade beverages will cost only a fraction of the price of their commercial counterparts and their quality will be far superior to the store-bought varieties.

Recipes for both dark and light beer are included here. The alcoholic content, by the way, will be much higher than that of commercial beer, so be prudent about your consumption at any one time.

Good table wines from grapes are available today at reasonable prices in most states, so I don't envision your making all the wine you consume or your giving up grape wines for fruit wines. The fruit wine suggestions given here may be only starters for you. I have selected them because they are wonderfully festive, allow for limited work space by calling for fairly small quantities of fruit, and give you the pleasure of working with good fresh fruit. Home winemaking from wine grapes is becoming a serious hobby for many people today, but wine grapes certainly are not available in all parts of the country, and personally, I am not much interested in using concentrates. For those who do wish to get more involved in the process of making more varieties of wine and home brew, a list of recommended books appears at the end of this chapter.

Most grape wines made today are fortified with sugar. All fruit wines need sugar to make them ferment properly. To my taste honey does not produce a wine as fine and subtle as those which are made with sugar, though honey makes wonderful beer (see page 78). It should be remembered, as the supreme rationale for using sugar, that if these products are made properly, all the sugar will be converted to alcohol and carbon dioxide.

The wine recipes are designed to produce all-purpose light wines to be used primarily as aperitifs, but they can also be used lightly with dinner menus, especially with fowl or fish. These wines will give you a feeling of great personal luxury as they are inexpensively elegant and great fun to make.

It is essential to note that Federal regulations and Internal Revenue law stipulate that any household may, without payment of tax, make 200 gallons or less of wine each year for personal use and *not for sale*, though the head of the family must register his intent. Each home winemaker should obtain Form 1541 from the U.S. Treasury Department, Internal Revenue Service, and send the completed form to the nearest regional office.

Wine: Recipes, Equipment, Method

The following recipes are each designed to make 1 gallon of wine. If you wish to double the recipe, you must double all the ingredients except the yeast as many of the wine yeast packages will activate 1 to 5 gallons of liquid. Check your yeast label.

Apricot Wine

> 5 pounds pitted apricots
> 8 cups sugar
> 7 pints water
> all-purpose wine yeast

Cherry Wine (tastes like a grape wine)

> 8 pounds black cherries (simply mash whole cherry, including pits)
> 5 cups sugar
> 7 pints water
> all-purpose wine yeast

Blackberry Wine

> 5 pounds blackberries
> 6 cups sugar
> 7 pints water
> all-purpose wine yeast

Raspberry Wine

> 4 pounds raspberries
> 5 cups sugar
> 7 pints water
> all-purpose wine yeast

Plum Wine

> 8 pounds ripe plums (mash with stones)
> 6 cups sugar
> 7 pints water
> burgundy wine yeast (this is a heavier wine)

Equipment

PRIMARY FERMENTER.   An earthenware crock is preferable, but a plastic pail is sufficient. (A polyethylene garbage pail is ecologically sound if you use it forever and pass it on to your children, though it is less aesthetic.) This container should be large enough to hold 2 or 3 gallons of liquid, depending on how much wine you want to make.

Another container of equal size is needed for straining the "must" (see page 176). I use my canning pan for this purpose.

WOODEN SPOON WITH A LONG HANDLE. For mixing, and you can use it for making beer, too.

	Dry Red Table Wine	Dry White Table Wine	Sweet Wine
Balling	23–24	22–23	28
Specific Gravity	1.095–1.099	1.090–1.095	1.118

Conversion Table: Specific Gravity at 69°F. to Balling
Assuming S. G. of water at 60°F. is unity

Degrees Balling	Specific Gravity	Degrees Balling	Specific Gravity	Degrees Balling	Specific Gravity
0.00	1.000	10.0	1.039	20.0	1.081
0.50	1.002	10.5	1.041	20.5	1.084
1.00	1.004	11.0	1.043	21.0	1.086
1.50	1.006	11.5	1.045	21.5	1.088
2.00	1.008	12.0	1.048	22.04	1.090
2.50	1.010	12.5	1.050	22.5	1.093
3.00	1.012	13.0	1.052	23.0	1.095
3.50	1.014	13.5	1.054	23.5	1.097
4.00	1.016	14.0	1.056	24.0	1.099
4.50	1.017	14.5	1.058	24.5	1.102
5.00	1.019	15.0	1.059	25.0	1.104
5.50	1.021	15.5	1.062	25.5	1.106
6.00	1.023	16.0	1.064	26.0	1.109
6.50	1.025	16.5	1.066	26.5	1.111
7.00	1.027	17.0	1.068	27.0	1.113
7.50	1.029	17.5	1.070	27.5	1.116
8.00	1.031	18.0	1.072	28.0	1.118
8.50	1.033	18.5	1.075	28.5	1.120
9.00	1.035	19.0	1.077	29.0	1.123
9.50	1.037	19.5	1.079	29.5	1.125

HYDROMETER OR SACCHAROMETER.   A hydrometer is basically an instrument for measuring the density of a liquid in relation to the density of water. In brewing, its purpose is to indicate the cessation of fermentation (when the sugar has converted to alcohol), since the lapse between total fermentation and bottling is crucial to prevent the beer from going flat. The hydrometer is a sealed glass tube with a weighted glass bulb at one end. It sinks as the sugar converts. *In winemaking*, a saccharometer is used to determine the sugar content in the primary must and to predict the alcohol content in the finished wine. Generally, sugar, when fermented, gives half its amount of alcohol by volume. Most hydrometers sold in the United States have tables for both beer and wine. Ask your hardware or winemaking supplier about the specific instrument he sells and be certain to get accurate instruction for its use. The wine recipes in this chapter call for definite amounts of sugar and, therefore, a hydrometer or saccharometer is unnecessary. If, however, you are making up your own recipes and are experimenting with amounts of sugar, it would be wise to learn to use these instruments. The two common scales in English-speaking countries are the (Brix) Balling Scale and the Specific Gravity Scale. Roughly calculated, these readings can serve as guides for the three major wine types, although some recipes list specific gravity readings, and in such cases the recipe should be followed.

GALLON JUGS.   Used for secondary fermentation. Buy from winemaker supply house or save from cider.

FERMENTATION LOCKS.   Winemaking suppliers have several different varieties and all work well. They are essential to the process of secondary fermentation since airborne bacteria are a great threat to good winemaking. These devices prevent air from entering the fermenting wine while allowing the carbon dioxide to escape. The locks should be filled to the marked line with metabisulphite solution (to make, see page 75). The gas will continue to bubble up through the liquid in the lock and cease with the completion of fermentation.

WINE YEAST.   This is definitely superior to baking yeast and can be obtained from any winemaking supply house. There are several varieties available and your choice will depend on the type of wine you are making. All recipes in this chapter except plum wine call for an all-purpose yeast. Other recipes that you may use for other kinds of wine will discuss yeast nutrients (which motivate action of yeast) and acid blends (which correct acid content). They are not required in the recipes given here.

CAMPDEN TABLETS.   These contain sodium metabisulphite (or potassium metabisulphite), which is also available in grain form from some druggists. The tablets can be obtained from any winemaking supply house. Based on the old sulphiting method of grape winemaking, where sulphur sticks are burned in the barrel to

74

keep away the spoiling bacteria, the tablets are dissolved in the must (see page 76) and release sulphur dioxide, which acts as a sterilizing agent. Not harmful, they are very important in making fruit wines if you don't want vinegar instead of wine.

POLYETHYLENE SHEETING.   A cover for a crock or pail when one or the other is used for fermentation.

SIPHON TUBING.   Four feet of surgical rubber or plastic tubing (available from winemaker supply houses) which is used to siphon off the fermented wine into the final bottles to avoid stirring up the bottom sediment.

BOTTLES.   Save all wine bottles and ask your friends to save theirs. You can buy bottles from the winemaker supply houses, but it is more resourceful to recycle.

CORKS.   It is wise to buy new wine corks from the suppliers, but you can use old ones if they are intact and clean.

CORKING DEVICE.   This, I think, is a necessity for tight corking. I recommend the Italian model which runs from nine to thirteen dollars. You will pay for it eventually with the money you save making your own wine. You can try soaking the corks for a couple of hours and shoving them into the bottles by hand, but it takes a lot of strength.

Follow the method below for all the recipes in this chapter. Once familiar with this procedure, you can use it as a guide in creating your own recipes.

It is important to choose fruits you like. I favor summer fruits and have selected those which are generally available in most parts of the United States. I have not tried using frozen fruits, but I assume that they would be perfectly suitable, providing the excess water is drained and sugar has not been added in the freezing process. All utensils should be carefully washed. Sterilization is important in making fruit wines, so it is wise to rinse all containers and utensils in a sulphiting solution. To make this solution, dilute 2 ounces of sodium metabisulphite or ½ Campden tablet (see *Equipment*) in ½ gallon of warm water.

Method

1. Crush fruit with wooden spoon or potato masher in the basic crock or pail, or in a small wine press if you have access to one. Add 1 quart of water which has been boiled and allowed to cool. Crush 1 Campden tablet (or 4 ounces of sodium metabisulphite or potassium metabisulphite powder) in ¼ cup of warm water and add to the pulp. Mix well, cover, and leave in a cool place for 24 hours. Stir 2 or 3 times during that period.

2. Strain through a clean cheesecloth or a fine muslin. Place the cloth over the top of an alternate container (the canning pan). Secure it by tying a string around the container and strain the pulp completely through the cloth. It is helpful to have two persons in on this step. This mixture is called a "must." Rinse the original container for use again in Step 3.

3. Boil ⅓ of the required sugar in ½ gallon of water for at least 1 minute and set aside to cool. (Keep track of the sugar you have used—it's wise to measure it out in advance.) When cool, add this to the must and return to the original container or transfer into sterilized gallon jugs. Add yeast, cover well, and set aside to begin fermentation. Here you can make a decision about what container you wish to use for the fermentation process. You can use the gallon jugs with fermentation locks (method described in Step 4) or you can use a crock or pail. The advantage of the gallon jugs is that you can cover the neck securely with a fermentation lock. If you use the crock or pail, you must cover it with a tight covering to keep out bacteria. I suggest a thin piece of polyethylene sheeting tied down securely with a string.

4. Ten days later scoop the top wine into a gallon jar (or siphon it into jars), leaving as much deposit as possible in the container. Boil another ⅓ of the sugar in 1 cup of water. When the sugar water is cool, add it to the jar. Fasten a fermentation lock filled with sulphiting solution tightly onto the jar and set in a warm place for 14 days. Next to a water heater is good.

5. After 14 days, boil the remaining sugar in the last 1 cup of water and add to the rest. Again fit the lock to the jar and set it in a

warm place until all fermentation has ceased and the wine is clear. Generally, the wine will clear before all the fermentation has ceased, but it is not unusual to wait a few weeks after fermentation to achieve truly clear wine. If clearing is slow, siphon the wine into another gallon bottle to settle for a while more. Keep the bottle corked again with the fermentation lock.

6. Finally, when all fermentation has ceased and the wine is clear, siphon the wine to the final bottles and cork. Set the gallon jar above the bottles, taking care not to jiggle the jar and upset the bottom sediment. Insert tubing gently into the jug an inch or so below liquid level and suck until wine appears in the tube. Pinch the end while you insert the tube into the bottle. Don't be rough with the tubing at any time or you may stir up the deposit. When you get near the sediment, stop the process. This siphoning process is called "racking." Cork in whatever manner you find best, but be certain the corks are in tightly and, if you put them in by hand, shave them off flush with the top of the bottle and double seal them with wax.

Wine should be stored on its side to keep the corks moist and prevent shrinkage. Instructions for improvising a wine rack are given in Chapter 6. Store in a relatively cool place that keeps an even temperature. Do not drink for *at least* three months. Storing your wine for six months, a year, or two years—if you can contain yourself—will greatly enhance its taste.

Beer: Recipes, Equipment, Method

Home-brewed beer tastes quite different from the commercial beer we know. It has less of a fizz carbonation and a heavier maltlike taste. It is comparable to some of the best imported beers.

Light Beer

1 3-pound can light beer malt extract (hopped)*
1 package brewer's light variety dry yeast
4½ pounds granulated sugar
1 package unflavored gelatin
5 gallons water

Dark Beer

1 3-pound can dark beer malt extract (hopped)
1 package brewer's dark variety dry yeast
8 cups honey (preferably unfiltered)
1 package unflavored gelatin
5 gallons water

Beer that is made with honey does not clear like beer that is made with sugar.

Equipment

5-gallon polyethylene container or crock.
Long-handled spoon.
Beer hydrometer (see winemaking equipment).
Four feet surgical rubber or siphon tubing (see winemaking equipment).
Beer, soft drink, or champagne bottles for capping. Screw-lid bottles can be used but I find that the seal isn't tight enough.
Capping device. This is an inexpensive device and necessary for capping.

---

* If hopped malt extract is unavailable, buy compressed hops from a supplier. General proportions are 2 ounces of compressed hops to 5 gallons of water.

Box of metal caps.

Malt. Malt comes dried or in syrup form in a can. There are hopped and unhopped malts, so if you are following a recipe, check the specifications for the proper type. Both recipes in this book call for hopped malt in the syrup form. (All canned malt extract is in a syrup form.)

Brewer's yeast. Use this type of fermentation yeast and not baker's yeast, which will give it a musty taste.

Gelatin. Used as a clearing or fining agent during fermentation.

Method

1. Dissolve sugar and malt in 2 gallons of hot (not boiling) water and stir until well mixed.

2. Add 3 gallons of cool water and stir in yeast. The liquid must be only lukewarm so the yeast will not die.

3. Stir, cover, and set in a warm place. Near the water heater is good.

4. After 2 to 3 days of fermentation, sprinkle the gelatin on top of the beer, *but do not stir.* The gelatin helps drop the sediment. Drop in the hydrometer and leave it there so that you can read it each day.

5. Observe the hydrometer and the action of the beer several times a day after the fifth day of fermentation. Beer is ready for bottling as the hydrometer reaches the B-mark, or 0%. The reading should coincide with the cessation of the fermentation, which occurs in approximately 7 days, depending on weather conditions. When the beer reaches this reading, it should be bottled within 5 or 6 hours to prevent it from going flat, although it is important not to bottle while there is still some action (bubbling) or the beer could blow the caps or shoot out like a geyser when it is opened.

6. When setting up to bottle, lift the beer very carefully above the bottles so that you do not stir up the sediment.

7. Insert the siphon tube a couple of inches into the beer. Suck on the other end of the tube until the beer rises in the tube, pinch the end, insert it into the bottle, and let it go. The beer will foam as you

are filling the bottles, so you will need to wait a little after filling and then fill the bottles a little more before capping. Stop the process an inch above the sediment. It is wise to have two persons in on this operation to keep an eye on the level of beer in relation to the sediment.

8. Cap and then store in a cool place like a garage or storeroom. Set the bottles upright as the beer will clear after it has been bottled for a while, leaving more sediment on the bottom.

9. Leave the beer alone for at least 2 weeks before drinking. Carefully pour the beer into glasses instead of drinking from the bottle to avoid the sediment.

Do not drink too much at one time—it's powerful!

ADDITIONAL READING

Anderson, Stanley, and Hull, Raymond. *The Art of Making Wine*. New York: Hawthorn Books, Inc.
Beadle, Leigh P. *Brew It Yourself.* New York: Farrar, Straus & Giroux, Inc.
Bravery, H. E. *Successful Wine-Making at Home*. New York: Gramercy Publishing Company.
Gennery-Taylor, Mrs. *Easy to Make Wine*. New York: Gramercy Publishing Company.
Wagner, Philip M. *American Wine and Wine Making*. New York: Alfred A. Knopf, Inc.

NOTE: Wine Art of America, 4324 Geary Blvd., San Francisco, California 94118, home winemaking and brewing suppliers, will send you a catalog on request. They have branches in major cities throughout the country.

CHAPTER 5

Simple Sewing
for the Home

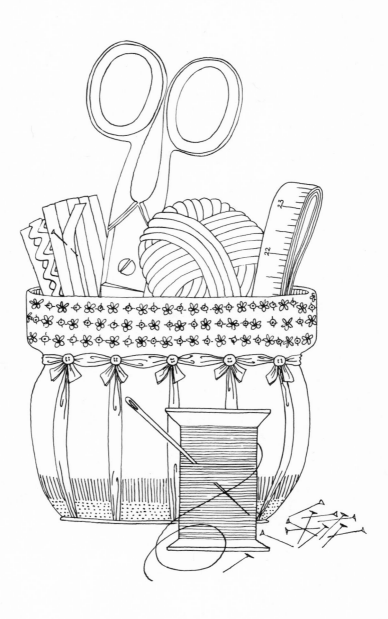

Fancy or plain, however; the fact remains that quilts seem to us symbolic of some of our finer human qualities. Perhaps the revival of interest is a hopeful sign for us all.

The Foxfire Book

A NEW AGE OF handicrafts has arrived. It has, in fact, been in full swing for several years in the counterculture, but in the last year or two the interest in this area of creative self-expression has gathered support from all corners of society. There is no question in my mind that this is one of the more positive changes in our culture, offering feasible and credible solutions to two basic and crucial human needs. The need for individual resourcefulness is truly as important as the necessity for creative self-expression. We are all aware of the escalating costs and the lack of durability of even the simple necessities for creature comfort. It is not surprising that, along with raising their own food, men, women, and children are learning to make clothing, shoes, and furniture. The return to such fundamental skills is a great boost to reusing and recycling discarded items.

All of the ideas and instructions in this chapter are primarily confined to practical, simple sewing for the home; but for those who are interested in more than the essential aesthetics of homemaking, such crafts as macramé, embroidery, crocheting, knitting, weaving, and needlepoint, a list of basic books appears at the end of the chapter.

Sewing Machines
Owning a sewing machine is not absolutely necessary for simple

sewing, but it certainly helps if you don't have the patience and precision for doing long, straight seams. There is an enormous range in price, performance, and capability in the available sewing machines. I have an old treadle machine which I bought at a garage sale for ten dollars. It only sews forward and has no extras, but the tension is terrific and it serves my limited needs nicely. It also pulls no electrical power. On the other hand, my sister has an expensive Swiss machine which does everything but select the fabric. But she sews professionally and can appreciate the many advantages of a versatile machine.

New and used sewing machines are readily available all over the country. There are always second-hand machines around. Watch the local papers and community bulletin boards. There are two basic kinds of machine, belt and gear-driven; the most expensive machines are gear-driven. They are infinitely superior for continual use, but there is a market for cheaper belt machines that will get only periodic use. It's sometimes difficult to distinguish the type by looking at the machine because newer model belt-driven machines are made with the belt inside the casing. If you invest in a new machine, check around carefully. If you live in a town of any size, try to find a person who repairs sewing machines only. Usually he will have repaired second-hand machines ready for resale. Another way to gain access to a sewing machine is to purchase one among several friends and share its use.

Draperies and Curtains

The idea of buying a ready-made drapery or curtain appalls me. Most commercial window coverings that are inexpensive are flimsy and unimaginative, and custom-made curtains are often too high-priced. Most window coverings involve only simple straight-seam sewing and the worst you can say about making them is that they are so easy they are boring. However, creating your own can be rewarding, since almost any type of fabric you may have on hand can be fashioned into a nice drapery or curtain.

Among the many styles is the traditional long drapery, which hangs and draws well. You can make it inexpensively from heavy, unbleached muslin with pleating tape sewn on top. I still prefer 100% cotton muslin and simply accept the fact that it will have to be ironed, but partly synthetic muslins that will wrinkle very little are now made. Pleater tape is purchased ready to use and has pockets for the pronged hooks to fit into. They must be attached to a traverse curtain rod, which is used for manipulating heavy draperies.

When you purchase the muslin, remember that the width for each drapery should be twice the width of your window, with an additional allowance for seams. For example, let us assume your window is 80 inches wide and the muslin is 45 inches wide. You should buy four pieces of muslin, each the length of the window plus an additional ½ yard for hems. This will also allow for an approximate 1½-inch shrinkage per yard. Calculate the amount before you buy, then divide the total amount by four and have the salesperson cut it in four equal lengths. This will make it easier to handle since you will want to machine wash the muslin in hot water and dry the material in a dryer before stitching. Later you will be able to wash the draperies without worry of shrinkage.

Now, sew two lengths together along one side, allowing only a ½-inch seam. This will allow you a 4-inch seam on each side of the drape. All of the seams running the length of the drapery require only turning once as they are the selvage edge (or mill edge) and will not ravel. Sewing teachers and my mother will instruct you to cut off the selvage. The reason is that the selvage can cause the seam to pucker and affect the line of the finished product. I, personally, don't worry about this and opt for the simpler method. If you do cut off the selvages, spread the seam and tack down the raw edges on each side of the seam by hand or by machine or use a French seam.

Press the seams after sewing. My mother always said the pressing was what distinguished a ready-made garment from a homemade one, although the quality of ready-made items has altered somewhat since her upbringing.

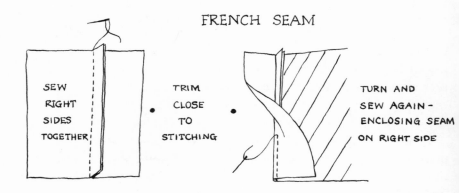

FRENCH SEAM

SEW
RIGHT
SIDES
TOGETHER

TRIM
CLOSE
TO
STITCHING

TURN AND
SEW AGAIN –
ENCLOSING SEAM
ON RIGHT SIDE

After completing the seams that join the widths, stitch the side hems. Then sew the tape on the top of the curtain. To do this, first turn an inch or so over and press to eliminate the raw edge, then turn once more and make a hem the width of the tape. Press, then pin on the tape and stitch all around. For the bottom hem, turn under twice, the same amount each time, press, and pin. A large hem adds weight to the finished drapery and makes it hang better. If your fabric store carries weights for drapery hems, buy one for each corner of your hem and sew them in the folded corner. If you put in the bottom hem by hand, the drapery will look and hang better. After one last pressing, you are ready to attach the hooks to the tape and hang your finished drapery. For those who have not put up a traverse rod, the directions are on the package.

Now, if you are more particular, are seeking a more professional look for your draperies, or wish to avoid certain fabrics' translucence, line them with a suitable light cotton. Ask about the percentage of shrinkage, but most lining fabrics will not have much shrinkage, for they are generally made from blends of dacron and cotton.

There are several ways to line a drapery. The simplest procedure is to sew the lengths of the muslin together to establish the necessary width and then do the same for the lining. Match the outside edges together with the right sides inside as if you were making a large bag, leaving the side edges open at the bottom enough to hem separately. Stitch the sides and the tops together, turn right-side out, and press well. Then sew the pleater tape on the top and press well. Hem the drapery and lining separately.

You can make any drapery or curtain with this method, but without pleater tape your fabric need be only 1½ times the width of the window, unless you want more fullness. There are several ways to attach curtains to the various types of rods. If you choose a traverse rod, you can simply attach the small brass hooks sold in the curtain rod section through the top hem of the curtain and then hook them on the rod. Plain brass rods are available for either clip-on or sew-on brass rings, which you attach to the curtain. My favorite combination is one with wooden rods, brackets, and rings. Wooden doweling for rods is available finished and unfinished in lumber yards and drapery shops. The lumber yard is often less expensive than a drapery shop; when buying the doweling at a lumber yard, have it cut the proper length and stain it yourself. The wooden brackets and rings can usually be purchased only at drapery shops and are available both unfinished and finished. Incidentally, if you have a lovely, heavy fabric, or one with an interesting pattern, you can often get away with using only one window width of fabric.

Of course rods can be hung at any height. Curtains that cover only three-quarters or the bottom half of the window still give privacy. In a kitchen, you can make a set of café curtains, which consist of a short ruffle, a foot or so in length, attached from one rod at the top of the window, and then a half-window curtain hung from the middle of the window on another rod, and perhaps divided in the center to be opened during the day. Fringe is a nice addition to café curtains.

All kinds of beautiful fabrics are available, some very expensive, but you will still save money and gain originality by sewing your window coverings yourself. All types of corduroy (wash first) make heavy, rich draperies, especially if they are lined. Burlap (never wash) is very attractive on wooden rods and rings, and you need only the width of the window. Indian bedspreads, available in import stores, hang very well from the clip-on gold rings because they are light. These are attractive, lined or unlined, although they fade rather quickly. For old houses with dark wood rooms that need light, hang short medieval trumpet banners from wooden rods that have been stained to match the walls. This is a very regal touch to tall windows.

I recently saw a simple, classic window covering that works well in the typical old city flat with two elongated windows situated next to each other, usually in the old parlor or dining area. These windows are the kind that often need warming, but not covering. Find a piece of regal fabric the exact width of the two windows and a yard longer than the window length. Turn ½ yard under and tack the curtain to the top of the window molding. Then gather the rest in soft folds in the center. Secure with a loose cummerbund of a complementary fabric, wide fancy braid, or a silk cord with tassels. You can add fringe to the top if you wish. Hem to your own preference.

You will get good mileage for the money if you use sheeting as a decorator fabric, especially for curtains and draperies. Sheets vary widely in price, and they come in every color and various designs. With an unerring sense of economy, one of my sisters dyed some old white sheets the color of her living room walls and hung them on brass rings. You may be more interested in using patterned sheeting in the bedroom, utilizing the lightweight fabric in a full, gathered style.

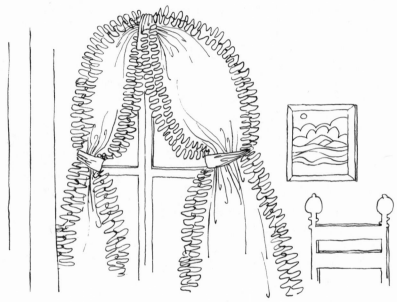

For example, if you have an arched window, split a double bed sheet in half vertically and seam the two ends together to make a continuous curtain that will extend around the entire arch. Take another sheet of the same size and make a ruffle to edge the entire curtain, along with 24-inch lengths to be used as tiebacks. Ruffle strips should be at least 8 inches wide and can be doubled for added richness.

Generally, a ruffle requires at least 1½ times the amount of fabric to which you are going to attach it. Gather the ruffles down the middle with a shirring foot on the machine, or make a double row of straight stitching using the longest stitch on your machine. Stop periodically and leave a long thread and start the stitch again. Then, when you have finished stitching, you can pull these various threads to gather into a ruffle. If you make a continuous line of stitching and try to gather it at only two ends, you run the risk of breaking the thread somewhere.

When you hang the curtain, fasten the center seam to the center top of the window frame and then attach the curtain all around the arc. Use one tieback to pull up the top center of the curtain, and the other two to pull back the curtain ⅓ of the way down on either side. This is a very sumptuous window covering, but quite inexpensive when made with sheets.

Actually, arched windows are lovely without curtains if they are in the main room of an old house where covering is not needed to shield the glare or guard privacy. It's nice to paint or stencil designs around the frame for a touch of Italian Renaissance. The arched window makes a good subject for broken glass designs (see page 7). Another possibility is to train ivy to grow around or up such a window frame. For narrow windows just next to the door, where the light is welcome, string some colored yarn vertically, pull it taut, and fasten to small brass hooks.

If you weave, or have a friend who does, try making flat window coverings of very light yarn. These can be rolled over a rod on top and hung loose, or secured at both top and bottom.

Sometimes a hard edge or tailored effect is desirable for a window area. One suggestion is to cover a plain window shade with fabric. This, of course, is also a good way to brighten up an old shade. The price of window shades being what they are these days, knowing how to cover an old one is worthwhile.

The most convenient method is the application of spray adhesive to the shade. It is best to bond cotton fabric to a cotton or linen shade. A spray adhesive will also work to bond a cotton fabric to a synthetic shade, but it is not recommended for joining a synthetic to a synthetic.

Begin by removing the shade from the roller. Pry up the staples carefully with a screwdriver. Measure the shade to determine how much fabric you will need. Cut the fabric exactly to the size of the shade, allowing 2 extra inches in length. Press the fabric carefully with a steam iron.

Spray the adhesive in 6- to 8-inch sections on the shade, starting at the bottom. Cover all this area with adhesive and allow to set about 2 minutes or the length of time specified by the directions on the can. Next smooth the fabric over the sprayed area, allowing the extra 2 inches of fabric to hang below the bottom of the shade. Then turn the shade over and spray the bottom area to receive the free 2 inches of fabric. Repeat this procedure to cover the entire shade and then reattach the shade to the roller. Add a pull at the bottom if you wish. Use a shell or a tassel or an old piece of jewelry or whatever.

A last suggestion for a window that needs the sunlight diffused, but not obscured, is to purchase an outdoor roll-up bamboo shade. I have one on my front window and it gives a beautiful slatted light in the late afternoon.

Curtains, of course, need not be limited to windows. If you have a doorway that doesn't really need a door, but occasionally demands separation, hang a curtain (East Indian spreads are perfect for this purpose) from a rod with brass clip-on hooks, or from doweling with wooden rings.

Couch Covers and Pillows

I have not seen many couches for which I would pay the listed price. Occasionally I see something special like the deep soft furniture that some friends brought from Holland, and I do like heavy Mediterranean bench couches if they have soft cushions. Usually I throw my couches together from old mattresses and day beds. At present I have a narrow day bed, minus the top mattress, set against a wall under a low window, and a mattress from a double bed placed

at a right angle to the bottom end of the day bed, so that the two form an "L." The long side of the mattress is up against a lovely old chest (a buffet that has had its legs shortened). The chest makes a back for numerous pillows. In all, the pillows add up to seventeen, and there could be more if I were not through with that part of the house for the time being.

For a couch cover on the narrow day bed, I have used a piece of interesting fabric a friend brought from the Caribbean. Neither end is hemmed, as they are not exposed, although the most you would need to finish would be the exposed sides. The mattress is covered with an Indian spread tucked under the bottom with hospital corners.

92

Another way to cover a bed couch is to box the corners and stitch them down on the machine. This technique works well when you are using both a box spring and mattress for a couch, and when you have a heavier cover like corduroy.

For a fine couch arrangement that doubles comfortably as a bed (that is, if you are going to sleep on your couch regularly, use this method for the health of your body), build a wooden box and platform (see pages 107–111) and buy a piece of foam rubber 4 to 6 inches thick for the mattress. During the day remove the night blankets and cover with a spread tucked under, an inexpensive cotton shag rug which your cat will love, and sprinkle with pillows. It's rather like sleeping in a loft and it's very good for your back.

If you have an old couch of a standard style with arms and a back, you can either teach yourself to reupholster (see book list at the end of Chapter 6) or cover the couch loosely with a rug. Any light fabric will slip and wrinkle and be a continual straightening problem. Inexpensive shag rugs, designed or varicolored, are attractive, as are any of the inexpensive imports (Indian, Spanish, Mexican serape). Even the domestic cotton version of the Oriental rug works well. I think the supreme throw of this nature is a Navaho blanket, although it tends to be much more expensive.

An abundance of pillows will warm and brighten a room quickly. I use cheap bed pillows stuffed with foam bits for bolsterlike pillows because they hold their shape. Quite often you can find them for one to two dollars at dime or discount stores. I cover these pillows in whatever print or solid fabric appeals to me and then make smaller, softer pillows of different shapes to throw in front of the others. These I stuff with kapok, which is soft and shapable (though it tends to shed and stick to things). Shredded foam, which is not as soft, is also good. Kapok and foam can be purchased in large bags from J. C. Penney, Sears, Roebuck, or fabric stores for about three dollars.

The easiest way to make a decorator pillow is to make a bag. Stitch up three sides, turn it right-side out, and stuff it with a ready-made bed pillow. Turn the remaining ends inside and stitch it with an overcast stitch. You can put in a zipper if you wish. Myself, I would rather take out the hand-stitching to wash the cover and stitch it up again. It only takes about five minutes to resew. But, if you are using a loose stuffing, it is best to make a pillow cover first out of cheap cotton, fill it with the stuffing, and then cover it with the outside cover. Actually, I change pillow covers about once a year, and that is why I don't bother with zippers.

I sometimes use the old covers for table napkins and quilts, or give them to someone else. Find inexpensive remnants for your pillow covers, or make them from old clothing articles. Bandana handkerchiefs make great pillows, especially against wood or on textured couch covers. If you use a plain fabric for a pillow cover, decorate it with a design cut from another fabric, a bird or a flower attached with an embroidery stitch around the edge. Trim such covering around the edge with a colorful braid or ribbon or large rickrack. A patchwork pillow is a great gift. If you have an oddly shaped piece of fabric, make a pillow of an off shape, since a combination of pillows of different shapes is effective. Still another way of obtaining variety is to use different prints for either side of the pillow.

Old bentwood chairs are very popular now. If you want to use them for dining chairs, add richness and warmth by making round cushions to cover the seats from one of the velvetlike synthetic fabrics. Secure the cushion to the back of the chair by adding ties made of fancy braid. Remove the cushions for more informal dining, or for children.

Napkins and Tablecloths

I consider cloth napkins within the category of necessary luxury. Because of the enormous amount of paper purchased annually, half of which is strewn all over the countryside, it seems to me a small bit of personal conservation to use cloth napkins, kitchen towels, and handkerchiefs. It might be argued that the weekly wash load is increased and negates the saving on paper, but I believe if people are aware of this, they will be more careful about the use of cloth items. I remember when I was a child my father would always request a cloth napkin for himself. He simply preferred it, as in the European tradition. The rest of the family used paper except for special occasions. He did, however, use his napkin for several meals before it was laundered and this, too, is a European tradition.

The most reasonable solution to the problem of excessive laundering is to get personal napkin rings for your immediate family and use the napkins again and again until they truly need laundering. A fairly large napkin is the best for family use, but company napkins can be smaller. The red and blue workman's handkerchiefs are excellent everyday napkins, and they are commonly sold in a packet of five for a dollar. Make napkins out of scraps and remnants, mix the sizes and shapes, and don't worry about matching. We Americans seem to love having everything match in assembly line fashion. Do as you would in mixing couch pillows.

The best fabric for tablecloths and napkins is 100% cotton, since cotton is more absorbent than other fabrics and does not hold stains as do many synthetics. Also, dish towels make good napkins and so, too, does a new or old traditional checkered tablecloth. Definitely do not discard what sewing scraps are not used up for napkins, however, because they can be used for quilts too. (Quilting will be discussed at the end of this chapter.)

To hem a napkin, simply turn under twice and stitch all around on the machine. It sometimes helps to press the hem with an iron first. After laundering, fold the napkins carefully and do not bother to iron them for, unless you are having a very elegant dinner, it is a discouraging waste of time and power. Part of my position on this is due to the memory of my first ironing responsibilities, napkins, handkerchiefs, aprons, and pillowcases. I keep a set of matching wash cloths to be used as napkins for chicken and less dainty foods. Small guest towels work well also.

Make a tablecloth like a big napkin, but you will undoubtedly wish to press in the hems as you go, and maybe even pin them. Since most cotton fabric is no wider than 45 inches, you will need to get two lengths and sew them together to get the necessary width. Then, proceed as with a napkin. For a nice tablecloth, do the hem by hand. For a round table, buy two lengths also, but before you make the center seam, take one length and fold it in half. Use a tape measure or yardstick as you would a compass to measure equal distances from one of the folded corners, and shape a quarter of a circle. Mark that quarter with pins, and cut. Use it for a pattern for the other length, and the halves of your circle will be equal. Then sew them down the center and hem.

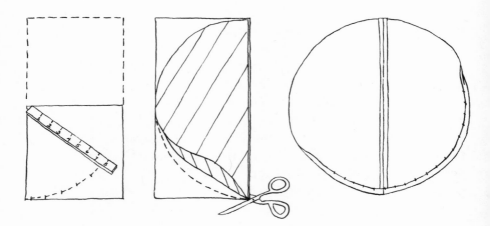

Since hemming a circle is tricky, the simplest procedure (which also yields the best-looking finished product) is to sew on fringe or ball fringe for a hem. If you have an impressive piece of material, it may be worth the effort to hand-stitch a hem, and leave it undecorated. Place mats can be made of fabric remnants also. Make a running stitch along the edge, or, if the fabric is a loose weave, pull out several of the horizontal threads to make a fringe and then run a machine stitch around to prevent more raveling. If you wish to give body to cotton place mats of a fairly light fabric, put them in a heavy starch solution after washing.

You might also have use for a runner, or long decorative cloth extending across the center of your table. I once had an elegant old walnut table in a rented house, but the center leaf was badly stained, and so when we were not using the table for eating, I laid a runner over the bad leaf. I had several made from different pieces of fabric, including a couple of inexpensive Mexican rebozos, which are long, narrow, and fringed on the ends. For dining, I used cotton runners and laid the place mats on top of the runner. No one ever had to look at the ugly leaf.

Wall Decorations

If walls must be painted, I favor white, off-white, or ivory, for the single purpose of creating a large canvas for a collection of different wall-hanging items. I prefer crowded walls, but even if you like sparse wall ornamentation, the white tones best accent anything you have hanging. Besides paintings and prints, wall decorations can be made from pieces of special fabrics, or even colorful remnants. Sew weights in the bottom corners and roll the top over a wooden or brass curtain rod and hang like a painting. If the fabric is light or you like frequent changes, simply use thumb tacks or upholstery tacks. Another way is to fashion your own designs from various fabrics, cut out, and glue onto burlap. Use your imagination here and you will be surprised at what you come up with. For macramé in progress, hang the piece on the wall and work on it at your leisure.

When you have a wall, especially a small wall, that seems to demand a break in the painted or wood surface, try covering it with fabric rather than wall paper. The strongest attraction for covering a wall in this way is the unlimited variety of prints and textures available today.

If you measure and cut carefully, you will not need to add any trimming around the edges of windows and doors or remove the molding around the edge of the wall. But if you are building or rebuilding a room, it is wise to attach the fabric before adding the molding. Use a good spray adhesive, a fabric with body (a sleazy

97

fabric will be hard to work with), care and patience. The effect is stunning!

One of my sisters has no closet in her bedroom. She hangs her clothes from hangers on hooks at various heights on the wall, along with belts, beads, bags, bracelets, and earrings. The room looks like something between a fashion showroom and a costume shop.

Rug Braiding

There are a number of creative ways to warm up the floors of a house without resorting to expensive carpeting. The last few years have brought a renewed interest in the Oriental patterned rugs. You don't have to invest in the real and priceless thing, though, as there are many beautiful and long-lasting imitations made in both jute and cotton. The former, made from a tough and fibrous plant, has an amazingly long life. Wool is beautiful, but much more expensive. Indian, Mexican, and Middle Eastern blankets make good rugs when set on a rug pad.

An old and reliable classic for the floor is the braided rug. Long associated with Early American furniture, it has for many years been duplicated in mass production with varying quality. If you have the taste for these long-lasting and warm rugs, here are some simple instructions for making your own. You don't have to be deep into the creative arts, because the craft, which improves with practice, is essentially relaxing and rewarding. In college I knew a girl whose father was a successful accountant who braided rugs for a hobby. Then I thought it was a bit unusual, but now I understand.

Wool is the most sensible fabric for braided rugs, cotton won't hold up, and synthetics are—well, synthetic. Wool is warm and will last forever. Utilize all old wools that are not too worn. Wools with a rougher, duller texture are best. Avoid the hard-finished fine wools that you find in men's suiting. They don't combine as well with other textures and are less interesting to work with or look at. It may be more difficult to find old wool garments since less wool is worn these days, but if you follow garage and rummage sales and frequent the Goodwill and second-hand stores, you will find plenty of used wool. Rip apart these items and wash in cold water before you begin to cut in strips.

The strips should be about 2 inches wide and as long as you can make them. They can be cut across the grain, but not diagonally. After you have cut a garment into strips, sew the strips together, end to end, with a diagonal seam (also known as a "bias seam"). To do this you overlap two strips at right angles and sew diagonally across the corner, either with a machine or by hand.

Cut away the excess triangular corner and use your iron to press open. When you have used up the entire item, fold each side of the strip inward about ½ inch, like commercial bias tape, and then fold the strip once more down the center. Your strip will then be four thicknesses.

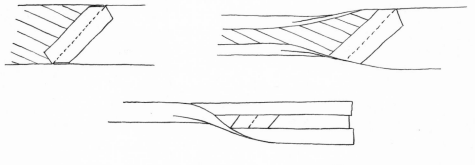

99

Secure the end with a safety pin and begin to roll the folded strip into a ball or onto a spool, folding the edges as you roll.

Don't attempt a large rug at first. Wait until you acquire the technique of braiding and, after all, let's see if it turns you on. To make a 2- × 3-foot rug, you need 3 pounds of finished balls. Since it seems to look better if the outer edges of the rug are of the darkest wool, start the center of your rug with three lighter-colored balls.

Turn under and hand-stitch the raw ends of three spools and pin them together. It's best to secure your strands to something to give tension to the braiding: for example, you might hang them over a nail or hook. Now start to braid. When braiding fabric for a rug, do not twist as you do with hair. The strips should be kept flat as you turn them. Continue braiding, and when one of the balls is finished attach a new ball the same way in which the first strands were joined.

The shape of the rug is your decision. The oval shape is the most common and functional. If you choose this shape, the length of the starting braid will determine the finished size of the floor covering: it is always the difference between the width and length of the completed rug. So, if your rug is to be 2 × 3 feet, you will need a 1-foot-long center braid. If you remember this rule, you will be able to plan your rug size without difficulty.

To sew the braid together, you should use a bodkin (a heavy, blunt needle to sew through loops) and heavy-duty cotton thread. Start by forming a U of the braid (2 feet), but making it lie flat at the turn.

Start at the end and sew through the loops of braid, but never through the fabric, so that the rug will always be reversible. As the rug is gaining shape, try to make the stitches on the body of the rug closer together than on the braid you are attaching. This practice is particularly necessary when you are making the corners for about the first ten rounds, so that you eliminate bunching or cupping. When making a round rug (which is one continuous corner), follow this suggestion every few inches in the beginning, and then only for each foot or so as the rug grows. To end your rug, sew the ends of the

100

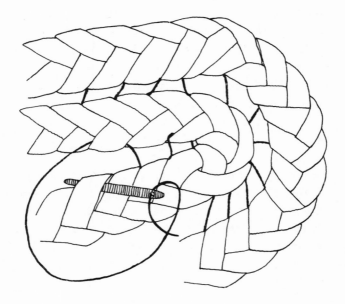

braid with an over-under stitch to prevent raveling and sew the braid to the rug, tapering it as much as possible and sewing it tightly. The end will show, but there are always quaint imperfections in any craft.

Another interesting idea for creating an area rug is to buy or beg carpet samples and remnants from your local carpet company. Use different colors, weaves, and textures, and arrange them on a piece of heavy canvas. Leave an extra few inches on the raw edge of the canvas for hemming. Glue down the pieces with a good mixture for fabric gluing. When the pieces are dry and secure, turn under the extra canvas and hem with a carpet thread.

Quilting

Quilting is an art and pastime as American as the Fourth of July. Though the origin is European, the images we have of quilts and quilting bees are thoroughly Early American. The actual practice of making the traditional quilt is much more complicated than one

101

might think. It is important to make it according to a particular set pattern: there are dozens of these patterns in any one area of the country alone. The value of the finished work depends on exact adherence to the pattern. My neighbor, who is quite elderly and whose hands are bent and stiff with arthritis, makes beautiful quilts with pieces of fabric no bigger than a postage stamp. She sews them together by hand and observes a pattern that specifies not only uniform size and design, but also set changes of color.

For the purpose of this basic chapter, I will confine the discussion to the easier and more common patchwork sewing. The popularity of this offhand pattern is evinced by the many articles of clothing you see in fabrics printed like patchwork, as well as boutique items made from pieces of actual patchwork. The ideas for using patchwork are endless: shirts, skirts, aprons, curtains, tablecloths, pillows, scarves, mufflers. One of my sisters made her four-year-old daughter patchwork coveralls. It is important to remember that all patchwork must be lined to be durable. It is also important to wash all scraps for your patchwork before you begin. Then, should there be a difference in fiber content, they will not shrink or tear in the finished item. If you are saving pieces for a quilt or just general patchwork, it is a good idea to make one item in the same or nearly the same type of fabric to give a uniform weight to the finished product. Or, if you use a variety of different fabrics, work out a pattern that balances.

The easiest and most solid way to make patchwork is to cut uniform pieces of the washed scraps and sew long strips of patches. It is wise to sew double seams for strength. You can sew these pieces by hand with small stitches, or by machine. After you have sewn several or many (you will have to calculate how large a piece of patchwork you need for your project), sew the strips together, also in double seams. If all the corners do not meet, do not worry, because it is more interesting that way. When you have finished this step, you can lay your pattern on the piece of patchwork and cut just as you would with any piece of fabric. Remember to make a lining for your patchwork items. Even I, with my informal sewing methods, cannot reconcile living with all those raw edges on the reverse side.

Now, if you are making a quilt, there are two methods I would recommend. The first is the kind you usually picture when you think of a quilt—a soft, down-filled, old-fashioned bed covering. For this style, you will need to make a case for the stuffing. I suggest using muslin for the back of the case because it is strong and inexpensive. Wash and dry it first. For filling there is no question that the dacron batting is far superior to cotton batting. The cotton tends to lump when it is washed and the dacron is much softer. Both come in long sheets on rolls and can be purchased from stores like J. C. Penney or Sears, Roebuck. Large, well-stocked fabric stores also carry batting.

Sew the muslin to the patchwork piece, also making double seams. Stitch only three sides. Lay the batting out on the floor and slip the case over it as you would over a pillow. Since it is a bit of a trick to get it in all the corners so that it is straight and lies flat in the case, proceed slowly and carefully. Like kapok, batting tends to shed and stick to things, so be prepared to clean up afterwards. When you have it fitted into the case, pin the open end and stitch it together. It is absolutely necessary to secure the batting inside the case so that it does not slip around. Stitch in crisscross patterns over the entire quilt, or in whatever design you want to make. This can be done by hand or machine as long as the stuffing is made secure.

The second way to make a quilt from your patchwork piece is to sew it to an old but not-too-worn blanket. I like to use army blankets, or 100% wool blankets: although this type of quilt is flat, it is very warm. Simply turn the edges of the patchwork piece under and stitch onto the blanket all around the edge. Doubly secure the patchwork to the blanket by stitching a design on top as you would for the stuffed quilt described above. Unless the blanket is old and has already been washed, you will want to dry clean a wool-backed quilt.

ADDITIONAL READING

Guild, Vera P. *Good Housekeeping New Complete Book of Needlework*. New York: Good Housekeeping Books.
Handcrafts: A Golden Hands Pattern Book. New York: Random House, Inc.
Martens, Rachael. *Modern Patchwork*. New York: Doubleday & Company, Inc.
100 Embroidery Stitches. New York: Charles Scribner's Sons.
Phillips, Mary Walker. *Step-by-Step Macramé*. New York: Golden Press.
Znamierowski, Nell. *Step-by-Step Weaving*. New York: Golden Press.

CHAPTER 6

Your Home: Basic Furnishings and Simple Repair

I built my house from barley rice, green pepper

walls, and water ice, tables of paper wood, windows

of light . . .

Into White, song by CAT STEVENS

THE MANIA FOR ready-made domestic items that followed the Second World War has reversed itself in recent years, and we have entered the do-it-yourself, make-do, how-to, reuse, and recycle era. Such resourcefulness, I feel, is exciting and essential.

The first part of this chapter is addressed to those who wish to gather a few simple ideas for making some home furnishings, both functional and aesthetic. The selections were chosen for their simplicity of construction and functionality, and because, I feel, these items are easily and beautifully combined with other pieces of furniture, both contemporary and antique. The overall effect of such decorating appeals to me as a pleasant blend inexpensively attained.

The following suggestions are especially to my liking because I prefer rather heavy, simple furniture built for action and wear, but with lots of color for warmth. I hope at least some of the items will be to your taste. Create your own variations and finish them to your degree of perfection.

Box Frame for Bed or Couch

As mentioned in Chapter 5, the box-frame couch or bed is easy and durable, and it looks terrific with a bright spread and multicolored pillows. The box style mentioned on page 93, where the cover is tucked in neatly and the redwood has lovely grain and color, is a style that requires only a minimum of sanding in order to look profes-

107

sional. The amount of finishing you do depends on your preferences. My young niece sleeps in a bed of this design, though her father sanded the sides smooth and even carved one side in a wave. He raised it two feet off the ground and fastened it to the wall (also wood) with chains. The effect is wonderful and it reminds me of the Swiss bedroom in the De Young Museum in San Francisco. You can use these directions for a couch in your main room for lounging or sleeping, or for sleeping in the bedroom. Directions are given for both double and single beds. Don't be discouraged by the different cuts of lumber; just take the directions to the lumberyard, where the clerks are always very helpful. It's a snap to make.

These directions are for two sizes, a 5-foot × 6-foot-6-inch frame and a 3-foot-4-inch × 6-foot-6-inch frame, but since the lumber and foam rubber mattress can be cut to order, you can change the size of the frame once you understand how to construct the basic form. (Polyfoam generally comes in 6-foot-4-inch lengths, although you can special order a longer piece.) When you put this type of couch frame in the living room to function as a couch, place it in a corner, if possible, and line the two walls with pillows.

Use either rough-sawn redwood or surfaced pine for the sides of the frame. Both are reasonable in price. (If you prefer redwood, I suggest that you sand the outside of your frame to avoid filling your guests with slivers of wood. Redwood splinters tend to infect easily.) You will need the following materials:

SINGLE BED (3-foot-4-inches × 6-foot-6 inches)

- 4 6-foot-4-inch-long 1 × 10 redwood or pine boards
- 4 3-foot-4-inch-long 1 × 10 redwood or pine boards
- 6 16-inch-long 4 × 4 fir boards
- 3 3-foot-2-inch-long 2 × 4 fir boards
- 1 6-foot-4-inch × 3-foot-2-inch piece of plywood, ⅝ inch thick
- 1 pound 8d galvanized nails
- 1 piece of 4- or 6-inch thick polyfoam, 6-foot-4-inches × 3-foot-2-inches

DOUBLE BED (5-foot × 6-foot-6-inches)

4 6-foot-4-inch-long 1 × 10 redwood or pine boards
4 5-foot-long 1 × 10 redwood or pine boards
8 16-inch-long 4 × 4 fir boards
3 4-foot-10-inch-long 2 × 4 fir boards
1 6-foot-4-inch × 4-foot piece of ⅜-inch-thick plywood and
    1 6-foot-4-inch × 10-inch strip (Plywood only comes in 4-foot-
    wide sheets, so you will need to add the extra 10-inch strip to
    obtain the necessary width.)
1 pound 8d galvanized nails
1 piece of 4- or 6-inch-thick polyfoam, 6-foot-4-inches long and
    4-foot-10-inches wide. This is the mattress and it is wonderful
    for your back

Proceed as follows to make a single bed or couch (use these same steps to make a double bed):

1. Place two of the 6-foot-4-inch-long boards beside each other to make a side 20 inches deep. Nail two of the 4 × 4's flush to the corners. These 4 × 4's make up the first part of the brace for the plywood. Repeat to make the other side of the frame.

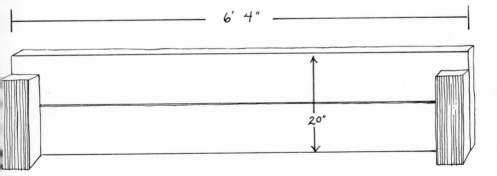

2. Nail two of the the 3-foot-4-inch-long boards to the end of each side on the outside of the 4 × 4's. You now have a rectangle 6-foot-6-inches long and 3-foot-4-inches wide.

109

3. Nail the remaining 4 × 4's to the center of each side of the frame, lining them up at the bottom. (When making a double bed, nail a 4 × 4 to the center of each end, too, for extra strength.)

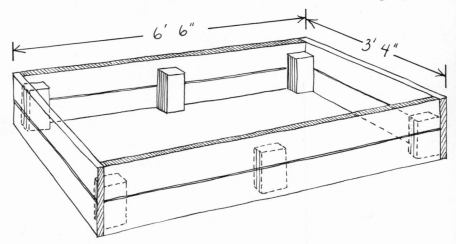

4. Position the 2 × 4's across each end and middle of the frame, so they rest flat on the 4 × 4's, and nail securely. This will make strong support for the plywood.

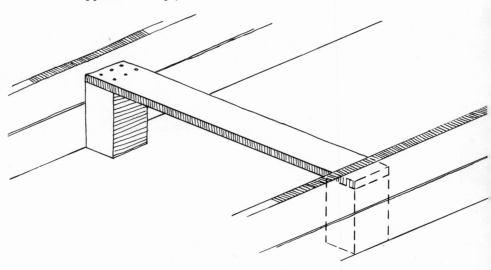

5. Lay the plywood across these braces and nail it down where the 2 × 4's rest on the 4 × 4's. You now have a platform for the polyfoam. Sand or stain the outside to your liking.

If you have a mattress you want to build around, measure it to determine the size frame to build. The inside dimensions of the frame should be the same as the mattress.

Coffee Tables

There are a number of good ideas floating around these days for easy construction of coffee tables. A popular idea is to cut down the legs of an old dining table or desk to make a low table with large surface area. I have an old dark maple dressing table that I use for an end table on which I keep plants. I cut the legs down so that it would fit next to a low day bed, and removed the arms for the skirt. (Remember those old dressing tables with skirts?) The finish is good, and the result is a rather interesting little table with its one small drawer and carved legs.

If you live near the seacoast, you may be able to hunt down an old hatch cover. It makes a wonderful and sturdy coffee table, with only a little light sanding and the addition of a support made from pieces of old porch beams or railroad ties. Hatch covers are very popular in the beach town where I live, and several restaurants have used them in their bars, covering the table top with resin to give a hard damage-proof finish. Personally, I find resined furniture too plastic.

For another lovely type of table, buy an inexpensive door from a building supply house (or use an old one). Select one with recessed sections, and inlay ceramic tiles to lie flush with the raised part of the door. Ceramic tiles are sold in masonry supply houses, and import stores carry Mexican tiles, which are quite reasonable. Place the tiles in the recessed sections, allowing ¼-inch spaces between the tiles and between the outer edges of the tiles and the wooden edge of the recessing. Use a good all-purpose glue or masonry adhesive to back the tile to the wood. Let the adhesive dry and fill in the sections with grout, the standard ceramic mortar. Follow the directions on the

111

package. Screw-on legs for tables can be purchased from building supply houses in any shape or size. A friend of mine attached very sturdy wooden legs to this type of table and uses it as a dining table. The tiles she chose are a beautiful delft blue and white, and directly over the table hangs a large lamp with an elaborate macramé shade.

If you have access to junkyards or live near a railroad yard, here is a suggestion for a sturdy house or patio table that is big enough for four people to eat around, Japanese style, sitting on cushions. You will need these supplies:

> 2 railroad ties in 4-foot lengths
> 3 4-foot-long 2 × 4 fir boards
> 16 4-foot-long 1 × 4 finished redwood boards
> 1 pound 7d and ½ pound 10d galvanized nails

Lay the railroad ties on their narrow sides and cross with the three 2 × 4's, which should be evenly spaced, and nail securely with 10d nails. Then, using 7d nails, nail twelve of the finished redwood 1 × 4's across the 2 × 4's to form the top surface. Rim with the remaining four 1 × 4's. Oil with linseed oil every day for a week, every week for a month, and every month for a year. Incidentally, do not leave oily rags in a tight closet or container as they are combustible.

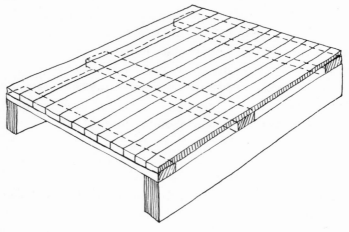

A Quickie Desk

A good working space can be assembled very quickly by using an inexpensive door for a desk top. In fact, I am typing this book on one I made. Buy a standard plywood door at the building supply house and have it cut to the length you desire for your desk. I suggest not more than 50 inches if you want to use only four legs. The same kind of screw-on leg that was recommended for the tile coffee table is fine for this desk. Have them cut to the height you want. The cut end of the desk can be covered with a wood veneer stripping. Alternatively, you can do as I have done to compensate for the plain style of the desk: take a colorful fabric and cover both ends from top to floor, bringing the fabric one foot around the front on each side. I stapled the fabric to the edge of the desk. Because these doors come in bland light plywood color, they are more attractive if they are stained and/or oiled. Of course, do this before you add the fabric. An even sturdier variation is to rest the door on a file cabinet, a bookcase, or wall brackets.

Refinishing Furniture

Furniture refinishing is so popular these days that even the least inclined person has done a piece or two. But for someone who is just getting started, I offer these suggestions. The book recommended at the end of the chapter is a good investment if you really want to get into it.

First, you must determine whether the wood is solid. The age of the piece and the style can be a reliable guide. Almost anything over fifty years old is solid. As furniture manufacturing increased, however, wood veneer became a common cover for soft woods, and these later pieces are least desirable for refinishing as you have to be very careful not to loosen the veneer.

To strip off old paint or varnish, use a good thick chemical paint remover. Follow the directions on the label carefully, and don't breathe the stuff. A metal scraper works best, and it is important to scrape with the grain. On the angled and convoluted areas you may

113

have to use a wire brush or even a toothbrush. It may take several applications to remove all the covering, but you can take off the last bit with sandpaper. Always sand with the grain of the wood. I think a medium or even fine grade of sandpaper is best to avoid making any gouges in the wood.

After you have sanded the piece to your satisfaction, oil or stain it. Linseed and warm mineral oil are good all-purpose oils. There are numerous stains available, though the best, according to an elderly friend of mine who has been in the business for years, is an analine dye which consists of a chemical base and alcohol (1 part chemical dye to 3 parts alcohol).

Now all this sounds easy, but you will find it is quite a job after you have started it. With a good piece of wood it is well worth the effort. If you are uncertain of the wood or the quality of a veneer and you have an ugly varnish to cover, it may be wiser to paint the piece one or several bright colors. To make the paint adhere, dip steel wool in ordinary household vinegar and scrub the entire piece with it. Always wipe any surface clean and dry before painting.

For unfinished furniture, the type of finish should be determined by the quality of the wood. Pine and birch are cheap and often look better painted, unless you feel the grain is nice enough to oil or stain. More expensive woods should really not be painted, or someday future owners will curse you when they begin to strip off the old paint to find the wood. Always sand unfinished furniture before you add any kind of finish or paint, and apply an undercoat when you intend to paint the piece. When you have one of those flashes of luck and find a piece of furniture made from good solid wood that has not been covered with old paint or an ugly varnish, simply sand it smooth and carefully fill any holes with wood putty. If the holes are large and putty shows from the color contrast, you can buy color markers for touching up spots, or you can use any nonwater base paints you happen to have on hand. Then oil or wax the article several times.

An effective polish for finished furniture was given to me by my mother. It is made with 2 tablespoons of olive oil and 4 tablespoons of vinegar to 1 quart of water. Mix them together and heat just until warm. Use it immediately: spread on furniture with clean cloth, wait five minutes, and polish with a soft cloth.

A Suggestion for Shelves

The addition of shelving to any room is pretty common practice. Aside from the student style of stacking odd pieces of lumber on bricks, cork, or cement blocks, the quickest and most convenient way I know to assemble a shelf is to buy adjustable brackets at a building supply house, where someone can tell you how to screw them to your wall and suggest a variety of wood from which to select the shelves. For the kitchen, however, where there is a need for closed shelf areas, 1-inch × 12-inch fir is good cheap shelving. Use the 1 × 12's for both the shelves and the siding. You will have to ascertain your wall's composition in order to choose the proper type of attachment. To locate the studs in your walls, pound the walls with a cloth-covered hammer (so you won't make gouges). It is unwise to attach anything heavy to a wall where there is no stud to hold it, but there are special bolts to use in the event you cannot find a stud. These are called molly bolts and come in several designs. Consult your hardware or building supply store for information and directions for using mollies.

In my kitchen, I have put up a simple boxlike construction with three shelves inside. It is nailed directly to the studs in the wall. For reinforcement of the second and third shelves I have added a strip of 1-inch × 2-inch fir to the underside of each, attaching it with wood screws to the boards. I oiled the shelves several times in the beginning and now can easily wipe them clean with a damp rag. I keep jars of grains as well as colorful pottery on them.

A Kitchen Cutting Board

Every kitchen needs a good cutting board. The problem for most of us is that the price of buying or even making a hardwood cutting board is out of our range. A good solution is to make one from

115

2-inch tongue-and-groove oak flooring, a procedure that is much easier than laminating thick oak or maple. To conserve funds, the Whole Earth Restaurant in Santa Cruz, California, made this type of cutting board in the early days of its existence. Now, three years later, it still functions—and it is artistically covered with vegetable juices.

Go to a floor company and have a clerk cut the length of flooring pieces you need. (You can cover an entire counter.) If your area is 2 feet deep, you will need twelve pieces of tongue, that is, one piece for every 2 inches. Mount the flooring on plywood for a detachable counter, unless, of course, you have an old counter and want to cover it permanently. Use small 4d or 5d galvanized nails and mount one piece at a time, toenailing (slanting) the nails through the grooves. I think it is best to use a good construction adhesive to secure the flooring doubly to the plywood and between the tongue and grooving.

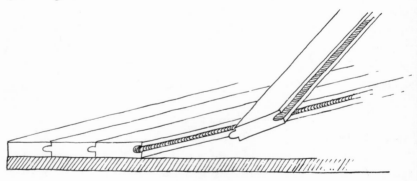

Toenailing the nails makes them invisible, but for amateur carpenters this method may be a little tricky. You can drive finishing nails straight through the top of the flooring and make it an easier project. A finishing nail has a small unobtrusive head that is countersunk after being pounded flat to the wood. To countersink a nail, you need a nail set, a small, inexpensive tool that drops the nail slightly below the surface of the wood.

Fill the holes with wood putty, and oil the entire top several times with mineral oil. To finish the edges, use oak molding on three sides to form a lip; finish the front side with wood veneer stripping. This material makes a most attractive and suitable counter, which you can also make into a table by adding legs and cross supports.

These directions are not exact because this idea can be adjusted for making either a counter or free-standing cutting board. Methods for assembling flooring vary, and your flooring clerk can offer you some hints.

Replacing Wood-Frame Screening

Who hasn't moved into an old house or apartment with at least one torn window or door screen? If they are the aluminum-sashed screens, chances are you will have to replace the entire screen, frame and all, or at least take it to a screening company. On an old house, however, the frames will probably be wooden. If so, simply remove the narrow molding that holds the screen in place. Use a small, wide-blade screwdriver, which you prod with a hammer, to lift the molding and pry under each nail from the screen side of the molding. If you are careful, you can lift out the small finishing nails and use everything again. Remove the screening, measure it, and cut the same amount to replace it. Attach the new screening with a staple gun (everyone needs a staple gun), pulling it tight as you staple. Cover the raw edge of the screen by reattaching the molding to the frame.

Wine Racks

Corked wine bottles should be stored on their sides when kept for any length of time, so that the wine keeps the cork moist, preventing it from shrinking and admitting air. Though numerous varieties of wine racks are available now at a wide range of prices, I feel obliged to make some suggestions in this area because of the chapter I have included on making wine and beer.

If you have a cool shelf somewhere, you can make a simple

wine-rack arrangement in one of several different ways. Large juice tins (the 48-ounce kind) can be laid on their sides to hold wine bottles. Cardboard mailing tubes, which are quite durable, can be used in the same way. If you don't have a shelf available, an old apple crate painted or decorated will serve as a frame for either tins or mailers. A very solid wine rack can be put together from concrete drain tiles. They can be stacked on top of one another in a cool place, such as a pantry or basement. Wine bottles with screw tops should be stored upright.

Candles and Candleholders

Candlemaking has become a popular project for making holiday gifts in the past few years, and it is an especially good one for children. Wax and molds can be purchased at most hobby and some specialty shops, but I have an even more resourceful suggestion. One of my good friends who lives in a lovely dark-wood Victorian house uses candles daily. To conserve on the cost of such a luxury, she buys them in import shops and recycles the leftover stubs. All year she saves candle ends and just before Christmas she melts them down to make new candles. She combines colors and creates beautiful new shades and shapes.

Candle wax should be melted in tin cans (coffee cans are good) in a saucepan of hot water over a flame. When the wax is melted into liquid, it is ready to be poured into molds. Do not overheat the wax or expose it to an open flame because it is highly flammable. Also, be careful while pouring, as burns from hot wax can be quite painful. Molds can be made out of any cardboard container if you grease the inside so that the candle can be removed easily after it cools. Waxed milk or cream cartons are excellent for molds, and they do not need to be greased. Ordinary household wax, too, is fine for making candles, and inside each package are directions, including instructions for making wicks from cotton thread. These wicks are not always successful, however, and consequently I recommend buying regular, treated candle wicking whenever possible. Weight the bottom of the wick by tying it to a penny or a thumbtack and placing it in the middle at the bottom of the mold. Tie the top of the wick to a knife or stick or pencil and lay it across the top of the mold to keep the wick steady while pouring the hot wax. When you wish to make layers of colors in a candle, pour one color at a time and let each layer set slightly before adding the next color layer. Sometimes you will find that your candle is drying with an airhole next to the wick. If this happens, carefully pour in a little more hot wax.

An impressive candleholder can be made from old ornate furniture legs, which you have sanded, stained, painted, torchburned, decorated, or whatever you can think of. I have several in my house, never tire of them, and constantly receive compliments on them. Also, old floor lamp stands, especially the type with several bulb arms, make lovely holders for large candles. The stands can be spray painted, collaged with paper, or antiqued, and the total effect is a majestic lighting arrangement. Old lamps also make nice stands for potted plants.

In Celebration of Small Things

Picture Framing and Matting

If you have a painting that you want to frame, the most costly route is to have the whole process done for you. You can save considerable money by doing the matting and framing yourself, even using a ready-made frame.

If you examine a professional picture frame, you will discover the corners are cut to 45-degree angles to achieve a 90-degree corner on the frame. This process is called mitering and the tool you need to do it accurately is a miter box. Without this or a rare knack for cutting angled corners that fit, you should abandon the attempt; otherwise the whole business can be highly frustrating. Also, if you have little affinity for carpentry in general, I would advise you to buy an inexpensive frame from the dime store, the lumber yard, or through standard mail-order catalogs, and paint or stain it yourself. Or, buy one of the new stainless-steel frames from an art store. These are great frames which come in pieces in a package and are easy to assemble. If you do want to construct your own frame, you can build a simple box frame from pine floor molding, paint or stain it, and nail the stretcher frame of the canvas to the box frame. A very nice frame of this design can be made by scorching the wood with a small propane torch (rented or borrowed). Smooth out the burned areas with a wire brush or steel wool and apply a good coat of ordinary paste floor wax. A frame of cheap pine gets a very nice, old, dark-wood look.

Mat board can be purchased from stationery and art supply stores in various grades, sizes, and colors. Use a mat knife (a single-edge blade) to cut a space slightly smaller than the picture itself. It is best to draw a guideline, since mat cutting is not easy. If you make a wrong cut or if the edge is rough, you can sand it smooth with fine sandpaper. The picture should be secured to the back of the mat board with brown mailing tape rather than masking tape, which tends to deteriorate more quickly. Fasten only the top of the picture, letting the rest hang free so that the picture will not buckle with time. This enclosure is sufficient without a frame, but if you intend to frame it, place the matted picture in the frame, back it with heavy cardboard, and secure it in place with small nails hammered at an angle into the back of the frame. Do not put printed cardboard next to the back of your picture, because the printing can bleed onto the picture. Seal the entire back of the cardboard to the frame with masking tape to keep out moisture. If the frame does not come with glass, have a piece of glass cut to fit the exact measurement of the inside of the frame. For a homemade frame lacking slots to keep the glass from falling forward, you can obtain small corner fasteners called glazing points to keep in the glass. They are attached to the front corners of the glass and frame. If you do assemble your own frame, the little gadgets that hold the corners of the frame together on the back are called Scotch lock fasteners.

The reason I go into such detail about matting is that I have some drawings and paintings I cherish, and I feel they should be well cared for. But if this all seems to be too much, staple your picture to the wall. I have done this many times with pictures from magazines, although if you are living in a rented house your landlord may not appreciate the multitude of staple holes in the wall.

Living in an age of increasing built-in obsolescence of consumer goods has forced even the very unmechanical me to develop a little command over the functional dilemmas of electricity and plumbing. It is no use moaning about automation when we *allow* our lives to be dominated by it. I have elected to limit the examples of home repairs as it is difficult to select just what might be problems in your home, since houses vary so greatly. Therefore, I have chosen a few problems I have run into in my own house, which is by no means modern.

Electricity

This area is fraught with multiple dangers for do-it-yourselfers. Any major repairing of an appliance or rewiring of a building

121

requires a good amount of expertise. Therefore, my feeling is that the first step toward handling electrical problems is to understand the phenomenon of electricity itself. It is amazing how many of us have absolutely no understanding of this vital force in our lives, one on which we are so dependent. I learned—so you can learn! And knowing will make you more self-sufficient.

Electricity as we receive it in our homes begins in generating plants or powerhouses. The giant machine turbines that produce power are moved by high-pressure steam, which is created by heating water in steam boilers, and are fueled by coal, natural gas, or fuel oil; or the turbines are located near natural configurations like Niagara Falls or man-made dams where the falling water turns them. In some smaller power plants, the generators may be driven directly by diesel engines or even by conventional gasoline engines. And of course now we are building many nuclear power plants in the United States. Electricity is distributed to residences and businesses along high-voltage lines for long distances, then stepped down for community use. This is all done through a network of transformers stationed along the power path from a generating plant to a house or business where electricity is supplied with either 120- or 240-volt service (or, in the old terminology, 110 or 220).

The flow of electricity through wires is somewhat analogous to the flow of water through pipes, with one major exception: electricity must operate in a cycle or it won't work. Your lighting, electric heat, and appliances are all interruptions in this flow, but all electrical wiring systems are designed to allow the flowing energy to return to its source so that the cycle does not run dangerously in all directions.

The flow of electricity to your house is regulated by a fusebox or the more modern circuit breaker. In each fuse the "hot" or "plus" wire carries the current to the switches and outlets and the neutral or "minus" wire returns the flow to the source (or fusebox). This cyclic process is called a circuit, and as the main current comes to your house through the meter, it is distributed through several sub-branches to diffuse and distribute the incoming power. The larger the house, the more items requiring electrical feeding and the more fuses or switches.

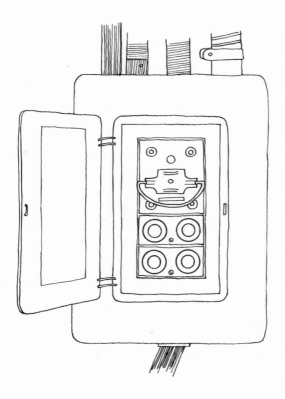

When there is an overload of power on a single circuit, caused by too many appliances, or a short in an appliance or a short circuit in the house wiring, the fuse "blows" and breaks the circuit. Or, if the system contains a circuit breaker, the switch automatically flips off. This is a warning to repair the appliance or to reduce the pull of electrical power in that area. It does no good to change a fuse or switch back the circuit unless the cause of the break in power is

123

corrected. It is difficult to diagnose faulty wiring within the house system, but you can check appliances by plugging them into different circuits. By all means, if you are *uncertain* about why your fuse has blown, call an electrician.

To change a fuse, look for the one where the small metal tab, visible through the transparent window of the fuse, has melted from the intense heat. *Be certain to buy the same size fuse.* It's best to keep several on hand. If you have a circuit-breaker arrangement, simply flip back the one switch that is out of alignment after the overload has been corrected. Some circuit-breaker arrangements have a main switch that will cut all the electricity coming to your house in the event of a power problem originating outside of your house. Use this main switch to turn off all the electricity when you are not certain which circuit is overloaded. It is a good idea to find out what outlets connect to each circuit in your house and keep a record of it. You do this by turning on everything and then removing fuses or "tripping" circuit breakers one at a time and noting which appliance or wall plug becomes inoperative.

We are all interested in the mysterious terms on utility bills and at the bottom of all appliances. Here is a brief explanation.

Volts, or *voltage,* is the measure of the push behind the electrical current. *Ohms* is the measure of the resistance of the wires or other electrical conductors through which electricity flows. Certain materials, like rubber and some plastics, do not conduct as easily as some metals but create resistance or barriers to the flow of electricity and for this reason are used as insulators around electric wires. *Amps,* or *amperes,* is the measure of the electricity that flows as a result of the push of voltage against the resistance of the conductors.

The electrical current coming through the wires heats the wire. The greater the current, the faster and hotter the flow.

The *watt* is the measure of energy used in the electrical circuit, and is computed by multiplying volts by amps. Thus a 15-amp circuit at 110 volts means the circuit can handle 1650 watts of electrical power. Because a watt is such a small quantity, engineers use the term kilowatt, which is 1000 watts of electricity. When your circuit has drawn a kilowatt for an hour, you have used 1 kilowatt-hour of energy, and the amount of wattage used is recorded on your watt-meter near the house. This meter is read each month by a utility worker, although experiments are under way to make it possible to send wattage figures by electronic waves to a central computer (again the powers of technology will remove another person from a job). The charges on your utility bill are relative to this process of measurement and depend on the watt power of your appliances, the amount of time they are kept on, and the utility company's charge for 1 kilowatt-hour of service. A 500-watt laundry iron used for one hour registers ½ kilowatt-hour on your electric meter. If the charge for 1 kilowatt-hour in your area is four cents, the hour of ironing will have cost two cents. Generally, however, the charges operate on a sliding scale determined by the number of hours used. (See Chapter 8 for more discussion on rates of power.)

Most major or large appliances and tools are factory equipped with a special grounding wire, which is simply an extra return wire, a safety measure to complement the return wire in the regular circuit (notice the three-prong plugs). This is to absorb any excess electrical current in the event of fault in the wiring or condensation in the metal housing of the appliance or tool. Generally, three-pronged wall outlets are installed in new houses today to handle the extra ground wire on big appliances. Most readers have come across the plastic adapters that act as a power bridge between the three-pronged plugs of large appliances and portable electrical items, and the old two-hole outlet. These adapters have a short ground wire with a metal tab on the end that attaches to the metal screw on the outlet for extra grounding. If you have further questions about the function of the grounding wires, it would be wise to phone a local electrician and let him explain it in his terms.

Before entering into instructions for electrical repairs, I issue a strong note of warning. Before checking or changing any wall switch or outlets, *cut off the supply of electrical current at the fusebox or*

125

circuit breaker. Unplug any lamp or electrical gadget you are working with. (Do not *ever* jam any metal items in plugs, outlets or switches.) Do not use power tools or large appliances that have not been grounded.

The following repairs are very common. If you make one or two, it will give you a new confidence. I then suggest you get the book on home repairs recommended at the end of the chapter for moving into this area in greater depth.

Repairing Cords

Many cords, especially lamp cords, now have their two-wire channels (the flow and the return) molded separately. These are known as zip cords.

To repair a worn section of cord, you will need to splice the good section of the old cord with the new cord. Begin by separating the two wires on the original cord. Then take a sharp knife and trim back the inside and outside insulation on each wire, being careful not to cut the wires. (This is called stripping the wires.) Allow at least an inch of exposed wire. Since there are many tiny wires inside each

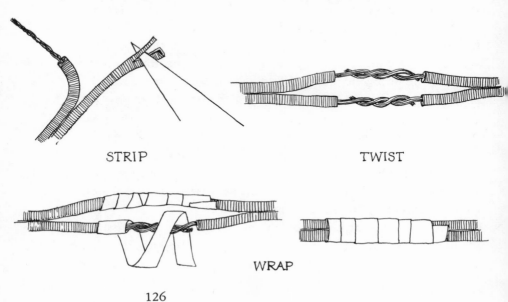

STRIP   TWIST

WRAP

insulation, it's best to twist each little set so they are easier to work with. To splice the facing wires, merely wind them around each other as smoothly as possible.

Then wrap insulation tape around each set of wires and tape them together.

Replacing a Faulty Plug

This is also the procedure for shortening a cord, though I think, if it is at all possible, you should retain the length of the cord. It may come in handy later, and for your present purpose all you have to do is wind up the excess securely in a hidden spot.

If you are replacing the variety of plug that holds the wires with screws, you can loosen the screws to remove the wires. If the old plug is made of molded plastic or rubber, just cut it off. Begin by stripping the wires as described in the instructions for repairing cords. In the screw plug, you pull the wires through and tie an electrician's knot, also called an underwriter's knot (see diagram), in the still-insulated

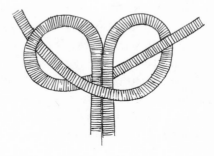

parts of the wire. This will later help secure the wires in case you inadvertently pull the cord too hard. Next, pull the cord back until it sits snugly between the two screws by the prongs. Take the separate bunches of wires and wrap them clockwise around the loosened terminal screws. Be sure to keep the bunches of wires separate and do not leave any loose strands as they would cause a short. In fact, curl the wire bunch once around the prong if you have enough exposed wire. This keeps it secure. Tighten the screws and replace the insulation face of the plug.

The clamp type of plug operates by the pressure of the lock in the center of the plug penetrating the insulation of the cord and making the connection. All you have to do to replace this type of plug is cut off the old plug and feed the cord through the outer part of the plug and through the clamp lock in the center. Open the lock to insert the cord. The cord does not have to be stripped or separated, but if the connection does not penetrate, you may have to make a small hole in the insulation where the contact points are.

Replacing a Table Lamp Socket

You will have a great feeling of pride when you discover you can rewire a table lamp. And it is an impressive gesture when you fix a friend's. First, make sure the lamp is unplugged. Then dismantle the lamp, removing the shade and bulb first. Separate the lamp socket by pressing on the side of the brass shell close to the U-shaped opening and then pulling. Sometimes the word *press* is stamped on the shell at the appropriate place. Remove the cardboard liner and expose the two wires and the binding screw terminals where they connect. Disconnect the wires. Next, loosen the small set screw located in the socket cap. Remove the cap by unscrewing it from the pipe nipple that projects up through the lamp base. Install the cap from the new socket in its place, tighten the set screw, wrap the wires clockwise around the terminals, tighten the screws, and reassemble the socket as shown in the diagram.

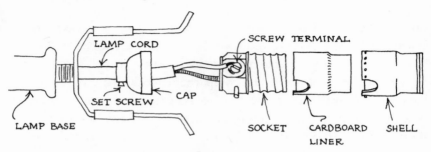

128

Adding or Repairing a Floor Lamp Socket-Switch

This type of switch is quite similar to the workings of a table lamp socket, though the cord enters at the opposite end. Remove the top of the socket by pressing and pulling off. Lift up the socket from the cardboard insulation and loosen the screws in the socket. Separate the cord and strip back the insulation as directed before, and wind each set of wires clockwise around each screw. Return the socket to the insulation and cover.

Repairing a Midwire Switch

Some new table lamps have no switch on the lamp. Instead, the flow of electricity is controlled by a midwire switch. These switches are, unfortunately, rather fragile, and getting stepped on and knocked around doesn't help their longevity. To replace one, remove the old switch by removing the snap bands or screws that hold the

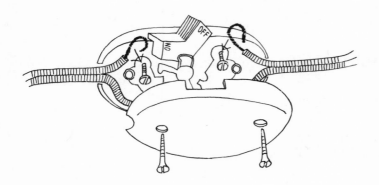

switch together. Open the new switch by removing the screws or nuts and bolts that hold it together. Fit the uncut lamp cord in the designated line for it, and take the cut parts of the cord and attach as you would when replacing a clamp-type plug (see page 128). You can follow this same procedure to install a midwire switch to a lamp that doesn't have one. You will just have to separate the channels of wire or the wire batches themselves if the cord isn't divided.

Replacing a Wall Switch

Here we are at the spookiest of electrical repairs, but since it is comforting to be able to do it, gather courage and begin. FIRST, FLIP OFF THE APPROPRIATE SWITCH ON THE CIRCUIT BREAKER OR REMOVE THE PROPER FUSE. Make sure you have cut the power to the correct area of the house. If you still feel nervous, cut all the power.

Unscrew the outer plates and then the switch itself by removing the top and bottom screws. When you see the wires, remember that the black wire is the hot wire and the white wire is the return wire (if the wires are other colors, call a local electrician and ask what the color code is in your area or kind of building). Sometimes you may find other wires, and their presence will mean that the switch you are working on handles more than one electrical item. Disconnect the wires, but take careful note of their original positions so that you will be able to reconnect them the same way on the new switch. (You *can* obtain a newer model which makes no sound when you turn it on and off. In fact, you will find a large variety to choose from.)

Attach the black wire to the dark side of the new switch and the white wire to the light side. Wrap them clockwise around the appropriate connections on the switch and tighten the screws. Return the switch to its space and reassemble to match the old switch. Turn on the power and try the switch. If it doesn't work, you have made a mistake. Try again, but *remember to turn the power off first.*

Replacing a Wall Outlet

The procedure is essentially the same as for the wall switch, though you may find more wires. If you see a red wire, it means the outlet is controlled by a wall switch. Connect all the wires in exactly the same way as they were in the old outlet.

If, however, you have just moved into the house and the electrical switches and outlets do not work, it may be that they are incorrectly connected rather than worn or faulty. Unless you have done wiring in the past and can spot a mistake, ask for help before creating a new wiring arrangement.

Water Heaters

Most of the new water heaters have directions on them that will instruct you on how to relight and regulate them. If the pilot goes out on an older model, I suggest that you call your utility company and ask it to send someone to check the heater. This is usually a free service. The gas company will also check your gas stove and heaters.

Plumbing

In order to establish a little structure to your plumbing lessons, you must first locate all the cut-off valves to your bathroom and kitchen fixtures. All toilets have a valve to shut off the water coming into the tank. Most reasonably new bathroom sinks will have separate valves for both hot and cold water. Some kitchen sinks do not have a valve directly under the pipes, and then you have to locate the main valve, which is often placed near the water meter. Always turn the valves clockwise to stop the flow of water into the fixture.

Plumbing repairs can be very problematic, so again I am going to stick with some simple suggestions with a reasonable guarantee for success on your first explorations. It is not so difficult to understand how water arrives and leaves a house, but the repair of plumbing facilities can be pretty tough. It takes certain tools and a little strength. (When a pipe burst under the bathroom sink recently, I knew where and how to turn off the valves, but they were so old and stuck that I had to run out and get my neighbor's help.) Most important, you need a great deal of self-control when the hardware store clerk tells you the part you are replacing is no longer manufactured and you will have to buy an entire new toilet-tank apparatus, or fixture, or house.

Now, if I have plunged you into the depths of discouragement, I know you will emerge with all your American ingenuity and determination to fix that leak. I have selected three common annoyances,

131

purposely avoiding toilet-tank problems, with the recommendation that you read the book on repairs cited at the end of the chapter if you are interested in proceeding further into the world of pipes. Also, if you have a friend who is a good plumber, ask him or her for some help with the toilet. The apparatus in the toilet tank is one of the chief rascals in the obsolescence of parts—though (and I think this is a beautiful example of creativity) when I first moved into my present house and decided to examine the toilet tank (I like to make a real acquaintance with my environment), I found a plastic coffee-can lid stuck on the mechanism that guides the arm of the ball float. It looked so stupid and out of place there, I took it off. And then the toilet started to run continually. I put it back and it stopped. See?

Clogged Drains

I am sure you have encountered problems with stopped-up bathroom sinks. And kitchen sinks are subject to all types of abuse. Avoid dumping egg whites, grease, coffee grounds, spoons, keys, and pet turtles down the drain. Except when an object has been dropped into the drain, the commercial drain cleaners or a plumber's helper will usually do the trick. Pay close attention to the directions on the can. These cleaners are highly caustic, and most of them should not be used until you remove any water standing in the basin and establish some drainage. I am positive that everyone in the twentieth century is familiar with the plumber's helper, or plunger. Every good citizen should have one accessible.

For what appears to be a simple clogged drain, start with a plunger. A little standing water is necessary for suction. Place the plunger over the drain, press down hard, and release quickly. Repeat this process several times. If the water in the sink does not begin to drain, remove whatever filtering apparatus controls the drainage. Most kitchen sinks have a drain basket, and some older bathroom sinks have a plug with the control device between the faucets. The plug itself extends down to the gooseneck of the pipe and you must look under the sink in back to find the connecting apparatus. There

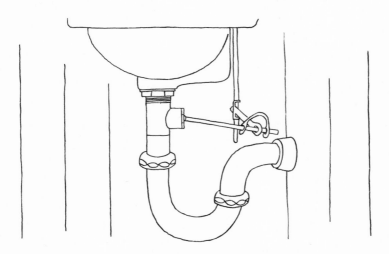

should be two rods held together with a nut and bolt. If you can disconnect these rods with a Crescent wrench, the plug will come out of the drain. If you cannot, bail out any standing water and use the drain cleaner and you should soon have results. Do not use a plunger or wrench after using a chemical drain cleaner.

Some newer sinks, especially in the kitchen, have a plug on the bottom side of the P-trap (the gooseneck pipe). If you can pull out or unscrew this plug and dig around in the pipe with a wire coat hanger, chances are you can dislocate the stoppage. If these methods do not work, borrow a pipe wrench and remove the P-trap. If your pipes are new, this may be the best way to get at the problem, and it is the only way to remove a fallen object. But in many old buildings the pipes are rusty and corroded and you run the risk of developing a leak in the joints of the pipe. Don't go overboard; you may have to call a plumber. If your pipes are in reasonably good shape, you will probably be able to retrieve fallen objects yourself. My sister frequently drops a contact lens down the drain; consequently she has become very proficient with a pipe wrench and one good eye.

The bathtub drain is not visible, so when it is clogged, a plumbing snake, which is a long piece of heavy wire, is necessary. (You can

rent one from a hardware store or plumbing company.) The idea is
to force the wire down the drain and shove the stoppage out from
the angles of the pipe. The process may require a lot of strength, and
my suggestion is to talk with a plumber before you get too involved
in a bathtub problem. (If there is any drainage at all, use of a drain
cleaner may be suggested.) It may also be necessary to get under the
building and remove a pipe, but before you tear up the floor, do
consider the plumber.

If your bathroom is not connected to a sewer line and you have a
toilet or tub that backs up or doesn't drain properly, the cause is
probably more complicated. The septic tank may need draining,
there may be roots in the drain line, or the leach line from the septic
tank may be clogged. Believe me, these jobs are heavy work and most
unpleasant. And you will need more than a pipe wrench.

Leaky Pipes and Faucets

Most often, leaks come from small pinholes in the pipes, from old
joints that no longer seal well because of age and loss of threading, or
from worn-out washers. Epoxy cement can be applied to small leaks,
especially on old pipes that still have a few years of use left. Consult
your hardware store for the best cement for this, and follow the
directions on the package. Obviously, the cement won't work on a
huge blowout. If your pipe should spring a big leak, turn off the
water, wipe the pipe itself dry, and try to determine the exact cause
of the problem. If the pipe is very old and you can see a crack or
hole, consider replacing the pipe. For this kind of work, consult the
Jackson Hand book in the reading list at the end of the chapter, or
call a plumber.

If the leak is at the joint of the P-trap on the drain pipe, remove
the P-trap with a pipe wrench. (If it crumbles in your hand, the root
of your difficulty is self-evident.) There is a device in each joint of the
P-trap called a slip-joint washer. If you are not familiar with the term
washer, this is a rubber or fiber disc placed in a metal joint to relieve
friction and prevent leakage where metal meets metal. A washer acts

134

as a seal and does get worn from pressure and age. Since the P-trap gets removed often enough to wear out these washers, you should check for this possibility if the leak is at the joint. Take the washer with you to the hardware store to get the right size. When you get into the repair habit, you will discover that an infinite number of sizes and designs of everything exist (new versions seemingly being developed by the minute).

You can buy little packages that contain an assortment of washers in the dime store. The washers in faucets fit over a screw inside to seal the flow of water from the pipe into the faucet. These washers, too, get worn and need to be replaced. Find the screw that secures the handle to the faucet and remove it. Then carefully loosen the handle, remove the washer, and take it to a hardware store to be matched. In fact, take along everything that comes loose so you can match the washer correctly. Be certain that you examine the order of the insides, so that you can reproduce it accurately. Newer faucets may require that the entire unit inside be replaced. Consult the hardware or plumbing sales clerk, and control your annoyance.

Washing Machines

My advice is to seek professional help when something goes wrong with your machine, or find someone who is inclined toward repairs in your community and exchange services (see Chapter 9). My mother always instructed us to shut off the water pipes (at the faucets) that control the flow of water into the machine when it was not in use. This relieves the pressure and lessens the chances of leaks in those joints.

There are many areas where the individual can avoid some expensive repairs in this machine-laden world. I personally am impressed with handy people. They make me feel more secure in an immediate sense, and I get a better feeling and encouragement for the future relationship between man and machine. I hope the reader will move into this world with the same feelings of hope and determination.

ADDITIONAL READING

Better Homes & Gardens Handyman's Book. New York: Bantam Books, Inc.

Hand, Jackson. *The Complete Book of Home Repair and Maintenance.* New York: Popular Sciences Library, Harper & Row, Publishers.

Johnston, James B., and The Sunset Editorial Staff. *Furniture Upholstery and Repair.* Menlo Park: Lane Magazine & Book Company.

Ward, Kay B. *The Feminine Fix-It Handbook: Everything You Need to Know to Do It Yourself.* New York: Grosset & Dunlap, Inc.

CHAPTER 7

Supermarket
Survival

Shortening, graham cracker crumbs, sugar, dextrose, non-fat dry milk, coconut, invert sugar, corn syrup solids, mono and di-glycerides, carboxymethyl cellulose, imitation vanilla flavor, salt, calcium carrageenan, tetrasodium pyrophosphate, disodium phosphate, artificial coloring, and water.

list of ingredients on the label of a
popular brand of frozen coconut cream pie

ANYONE WHO has daydreamed through the check-out line in the supermarket, watching shopping carts in front and behind, can tell you how America eats. I, frankly, am a supermarket buff. I spend a great deal of time in two of the major supermarkets in town, studying new products, reading labels, and trying to decode dating numbers. I have made friends with the grocers and butchers, and from time to time we have arguments over products and pricing. I eye a lot of shopping carts, too, and, in spite of all the looking I do, I am still appalled by what people will buy to feed themselves and their families.

In the past few years many Americans have been reevaluating their basic diet, and great dispute continues over the quality of food in the United States. The value of returning to unprocessed simple foods is explained briefly in the introduction to *Whole Earth Cook Book* and in many other books and magazines. In short, a revival of the old-fashioned simple diet is in progress. The purpose of this chapter is to assist the everyday shopper in the American supermarket in selecting the best nutritional values, regardless of advertising claims and lures. Even though there are many natural food stores, organic produce stands, food co-ops and conspiracies (see Chapter 9), and home gardens, most Americans still rely on the supermarket. In most countries and the United States of the past, a trip to the food market was a social experience as well as a necessity. I would like to see a

139

revival of the pleasures of marketing so that the socialization and the habit of discriminatory buying become a part of the daily celebration of modern living.

Since this book is in part a statement on the necessity of cutting back in consumption, and because the grocery industry turns out one-tenth of the gross national product, according to figures provided by Consumers Union, no one eating today can afford not to develop a healthy skepticism and discrimination in food selection. Just call it a sense of supermarket survival.

From the business person's viewpoint, the large profits are not in basic foods. Today the big money is in making snack items out of inexpensive ingredients and chemicals. Cereals, instant meals, goodies, and pop have thoroughly clogged the nutritional wheel, and protein sources, fresh fruits, and vegetables in their basic forms are steadily losing their essential place in the American diet. Technological mass production has infiltrated the food business for the same economic and psychological reasons it has penetrated every other aspect of the production world—expediency and profit. An army of designers now creates new food items daily, feeding and reinforcing our weakness for variety (think of "chocolate oatmeal") rather than nutritional needs. Consider the volume of food advertising on television that reaches children. If you look at any home-making magazine for women and calculate the percentage of copy devoted to food ads, and if you recall the numbers of recipe handouts in home economic classes and food sections of newspapers from companies pushing their products, you will realize how many channels the food business has cut into our lives. The industry's handsome offers for the endorsement of its products have induced well-known names to make unsubstantiated claims about the nutritional excellence of the products. Then there is the trading stamp trap, which is everywhere; but surely the worst act of advertising trickery is the "contest" that requires the participant to make a dish from a manufacturer's product or products. Naturally the winner is the one who uses the highest number of that company's products.

Again, to understand the food business, it is important to realize that the greater part of this industry has concentrated itself into a relatively small number of giant corporations that have emerged since the Second World War by swallowing up the small companies. They have created a market condition whereby they have, by a kind of gentlemanly agreement among themselves, kept food prices high and created false needs by appealing to our laziness and boredom and by conditioning our desires with convenience foods.

Although a great deal of money is poured into design, advertising, and packaging, the ingredients are cheap and contain little real food. Foods that entail a high overhead for the industry, such as quality meats, dairy products, and fresh produce, also have a high ratio of perishability and are not profit makers. The nonfood foods are profitable not only because of their basic ingredients and chemically induced long life, but because a company can play with them, first by constantly changing the sizes and designs of the packages, then by altering flavorings to create new products. And how can a consumer identify the items with a regular price if all of these changes are taking place? Surely one reason prices can be so inconstant is that basically the consumer does not think of these items as necessary foods, but as luxury substitutes for "ordinary" food. We purchase with a kind of guilt or childlike fascination, without questioning the price. Everyone laments when milk goes up, but few say much of anything when a frozen dinner increases in price. Probably this is true, too, because there is so much variety among these nonfood foods that one would be dizzy trying to remember all the prices. Milk and eggs and meat are always milk and eggs and meat, and we remain more familiar with their prices.

These nonfoods are plainly a significant part of the American diet since it has been estimated that 35% of the national food budget is wasted on convenience foods. Visualize the layout of your local supermarket. One of the markets in which I shop contains seventy varieties of dry cereal alone. Actually, it's hard to fix a price to any food. Meat and staples are the items from which "specials" are selected. And generally the specials are rotated slightly among the various chains to give the appearance of competition, but, in fact, they are only promotional devices. Sometimes the loss on specials is shared by the manufacturer, but more often there are compensating mark-ups on other items, especially those in the high margin bracket. There are several standard price devices to make the consumer "think cheaper," such as prices that end in 9, or items that are sold in multiples like 2 for 29, or 3 for 79. Of course the savings are much smaller to the individual consumer than the increase in dollar volume realized by the store. And such devices encourage overconsumption. The custom of unit pricing, too, has become confusing to the shopper. Although it is basically a good idea, it is hard for the consumer to shop in one store where there is unit pricing (the price is based on pounds and ounces), and then go to another store where the price is determined by the item. It is difficult to make comparisons in price because of the enormous selection of sizes, and while one item may be more expensive in unit price at market X than at nonunit price market Y, another item may be cheaper.

The grocery chains, like other types of large corporations, have been subject to constant mergers over recent years so that some of their holdings consist of businesses outside food. At the same time, many nonfood corporations are tied financially to farming. It does appear as if big business is one happy family in this country, but unfortunately the marriages and offspring are created in an atmosphere of constant concern for self-protection and profit. Because of this mutual commitment to such behavior, corporations assist one another by not creating competitive threats to the escalating cost of food.

With such awesome lack of responsibility in the food industry, is it any surprise that the natural food movement is being corrupted and compromised also? Can we be shocked to see "organic" stamped across the old label on a bottle of the same apple juice, the price now twenty cents higher, or to see a major bread company come out with an "Earth" or "Ecology" bread, although the same company has not bothered to remove any of its less healthful products from the shelf. Pure food products, so separated from the ordinary market stock for so long, and long considered faddish by many, are part of the "new consciousness" for many others. Some reputable companies are becoming more concerned about putting out good, nutritional products, but the usual profitmongers are having a field day in exploiting the so-called "natural food" idea.

The problem of organic phonies has not gone unnoticed by the people most involved in the natural foods movement. In the middle of 1971, Rodale Press, of Emmaus, Pennsylvania, set up a program of certification for organic farmers that establishes safeguards against false claims of "organicity" and offers guidelines for those who wish to involve themselves in farming the natural way. The program, which began in California and has spread throughout the country, continues to gather more farmers. This type of program helps discourage charlatans and increases the credibility of the reputable natural food companies.

Unfortunately, there has been no such response from governmental agencies such as the USDA, FDA, and HEW, which, though authorized to check on the indiscretions of the food industry, are generally slow to act upon charges of irresponsibility. Legislation designed to give the consumer some representation in these agencies has been so greatly watered down by the time it reaches the Senate that the consumer can count on but little power in the near future; yet the food industry is well represented by a powerful lobby. Meanwhile, by its very lack of assertion in protecting the American consumer, the government—once considered to be the regulator of business—is now a kind of silent partner, especially in the food and drug business. With all this in mind and very little improvement in sight, the consumer has no other choice but to become wiser.

A word about labeling before we move into the market. Most shoppers have probably noticed a coded date on certain products, especially those which require refrigeration. Unfortunately, the code is code, designed for market personnel rather than the consumer

143

—and it is usually unreadably smeared. A large number of chain markets are now marking products with a "pull" date for the consumer (as is done for baby formulas, which were exposed by a study showing quantities of out-of-date formula still being sold). Some mayonnaise and peanut butter brands are carrying a pull date on their labels, because of the problem of oil rancidity, but most manufacturers have elected to remain mysterious about their codes as well as the reasons for the dates.

Certainly there is a great variety of date codes: a pack date, the date when the food was processed or packaged; a shelf life date, the length of time the food will remain in good quality after the pack date; a freshness date, the last day you can expect the food to be at its best (this should be set before the shelf life date so that the consumer would have some shelf life at home); an expiration date, which, like the freshness date, is especially important in dairy products; and the shelf display date, which would be the date the food is put on display, and used primarily by store personnel for stock rotation. Because of the many different reasons for these dates, it is virtually impossible for the consumer to get any real idea of the freshness of a product. Many people pick from the back of the shelf if the stock is full, assuming that the clerk has put the older product up front so that it will be sold first. But who knows? Maybe the clerks are aware of this action and have reversed the whole procedure. Very little has been published in the major media on the freshness of foods in the market. It seems to me the most sensible suggestion would be to establish uniform federal regulations for handling and storing all foods with the slightest possibility of perishability. At the same time it is not too much to ask of the manufacturer to put a clear pull date in full view on the package.

Now, let's go into the market.

In my supermarket, the first aisle is the refrigeration case containing dairy products. I buy fertile eggs, though they are more expensive. I was raised on them and notice a marked improvement in the taste over nonfertile cold-storage eggs. California supermarkets

144

are stocking fertile eggs, but for people living in other states where they are unavailable except in natural food stores, I recommend choosing a grade AA from an egg farmer who is geographically close, in hopes that the storage time will be less. The grade, incidentally, refers to freshness, as determined by the position of the yolk in the white.

The dairy section is the place to request information on dating. Ask the clerk to give you some assistance in decoding numbers. When you purchase either domestic or imported cheese, consider the possibility of bacterial contamination in the plastic vacuum. (It's best to buy these foods in the delicatessen section where they are sold in bulk, and probably you will find them to be anywhere from five to ten cents cheaper per pound.) Never use any cheese whose package

145

has expanded. It is a sure sign of contamination, so take it back immediately and make a fuss. The same advice applies to all vacuum-packed refrigerated foods.

Except for "specials," processed and packaged meats cost from five cents to one dollar more than the same meats bought from the butcher. I cannot conscientiously recommend any processed meats, which contain a host of additives, especially sodium nitrite, which is considered harmful even by the conservative USDA. If you must buy these items, go to the butcher or deli; don't pay extra for chemicals and possible contamination in *packaging*.

Also, I don't recommend any of the nondairy substitutes or jars of cheese spreads, which contain preservatives. Even if you must avoid butterfat, you will only be substituting one health problem for another. Choose milk from the closest dairy and, again, investigate the dating codes. At one time there were margarines on the market that did not contain chemical preservatives. Unfortunately, now they are available only in natural food stores and are considerably more expensive. I personally buy unsalted butter and use it sparingly.

I am now passing the soft-drink refrigerators. I always pass by this section as I consider pop the supreme nonfood and the great tooth killer. When I lived in Mexico, I was staggered by the amount of decay in the mouths of the children of my village since I knew that the lime used in the making of corn tortillas usually gave the Mexican people good teeth. Then I found out that the great boom in the soda pop industry had canceled the good effects of the basic diet.

The next stop is the shelf containing grains, legumes, and pastas. Here we find another example of price discrepancy and an artful and impressive display of more nonfoods. The past few years have seen an incredible number of rice and pasta dinner mixes appearing on the market. Consumers are trapped by the pleasing pictures (food photography is a big part of the industry) and, of course, by the sheer convenience. If you opt for time saving, you may not be talked out of these foods, but please pay attention to the prices per pound. In

my supermarket, the price of both white rice and the more nutritional brown rice in the package runs from twenty to twenty-four cents
per pound, depending on the package size. Any of the rice dishes in
packages run from eighty cents to $1.00 per pound, which is quite a
bit to pay for a few dried herbs or spices, some chemicals, and more
processing. Various pastas alone are twenty-five to thirty cents per
pound, but the packaged dinners with dry sauce mix and spices
average $1.50 per pound, as do the packages of creamed potato
dishes. Even the mashed potatoes are ninety cents a pound and,
though they are dehydrated, consider the difference between a
package of those and a sack of potatoes at ten pounds for fifty-nine
cents. Have you ever priced potato chips by the pound? They are no
less than ninety cents per pound in my market, and that is the
cheapest brand.

Turning around to the cereal section, we are overwhelmed by the
quantity. As I mentioned, there are seventy different dry varieties in
my market and there are a dozen or so more in existence. Of these
seventy, there are only six that do not contain preservatives, and
twenty-eight are sugar-coated. Also, ugh, not only are they sugar-
coated, but they are sprinkled with marshmallows, chocolate, fruit
flavorings and colorings. The idea of pink frosted cornflakes for
breakfast appeals to me about as much as Christmas wrapping
would, but American children have been conditioned differently.

A major argument against dry cereals is the relative food value
(see chart on page 149). For the budget-minded family, the cost is
certainly prohibitive; the price for the extra sugar hardly makes up
for the convenience of not having to lift the spoon out of the sugar
bowl. Pink frosted cornflakes are forty-nine cents for ten ounces,
while regular cornflakes are thirty-three cents for twelve ounces. In
fact, all the sugared cereals charge dearly for the sweetening. I feel
that the big boom in cereal sales in the last fifteen years is due to the
constant changes in the packaging and the continual new versions.
I don't believe any child continues to love the same brand forever.

The industry, to maintain its profits, must devise constant varia-

tions in advertising as well as content. For example, during this last trip by the cereals, I noticed a couple of the old stand-bys had revised the pictures on their boxes so that the cereal grains looked much larger, the colors were different, more earthy, and the background was changed—hence, a new cereal. In the line of blow-ups, it's interesting to note that the cereals "shot from guns" are steam exploded to eight times their normal size. Compute how much nutrition you will receive from a bowl of puffed grain which actually contains one-eighth the amount of food value it appears to have. Think also about the price per pound in relation to the protein content. One would be better off to have a bowl of rice. Anyway we look at it, dry cereal has little value in today's diet or food budget. There are, however, several good hot cereals on the market, but the proportion to cold cereals is very small. Now the manufacturers are beginning to make a few flavored variations of the hot oat and wheat basics. Still, this is one area where you can get good breakfast protein with relatively few chemicals.

The chemical explosion and outrageous pricing occur also with the packaged dry baking mixes, only here the consumer has to do some of the work and add other foods like eggs and milk, which are the most expensive parts of baking. Aside from the nutritionless refinement of these mixes, the limited budget suffers.

COMPARATIVE FOOD VALUES PER SERVING OF REPRESENTATIVE CEREALS AND BREAKFAST FOODS*

	Cost Per Serving**	Pro-tein	Cal-cium	Iron	Thia-mine	Ribo-flavin	Niacin
Plain Oatmeal	1.5¢	4.0	15.0	1.3	.17	.04	.28
Muffin (1.7 oz.)	1.5	4.0	74.0	.7	.08	.11	.7
Farina	1.7	3.2	7.1	.8	.1	.075	1.0
Bread, enriched (1 slice)	1.7	2.5	23.8	.7	.07	.06	.68
Pancakes (2) (1.1 oz.)	2.0	2.4	127.5	.9	.125	.095	.8
Corn Flakes, plain	2.4	2.2	4.8	.4	.12	.02	.58
Bran Flakes, 40%	2.8	2.9	20.0	1.25	.1	.05	1.7
Cream of Rice	2.9	1.7	2.6	1.5	.12	.03	1.65
Shredded Wheat	3.0	2.8	12.2	.9	.06	.03	1.25
Wheat Flakes	3.3	2.9	11.6	1.25	.18	.04	1.4
Bran Flakes w/raisins	3.3	2.4	16.0	1.1	.09	.04	1.5
Oats, puffed	3.8	3.4	50.0	1.3	.28	.05	.5
Corn Flakes, sugar frosted	3.8	1.25	3.4	2.8	.12	.01	.5
Milk (½ cup)	4.0	4.8	146.0	.06	.04	.21	.09
Rice Flakes	4.2	1.7	8.2	.5	.1	.01	1.5
Oats, puffed w/sugar	4.4	1.9	20.0	1.25	.29	.03	.5
Egg (2 oz.)	5.0	6.5	27.25	1.2	5.25	.15	.025
Puffed Wheat w/sugar & honey	5.0	1.7	7.4	.94	.14	.05	1.8
Cream of Wheat (1.25 oz.) w/apples, cinnamon	5.6	2.2	n.a.	12.0	.15	.08	1.1
Puffed Rice	6.0	1.7	6.7	.5	.125	.01	1.25

	Cost Per Serving**	Pro- tein	Cal- cium	Iron	Thia- mine	Ribo- flavin	Niacin
Oatmeal (1.12 oz.)							
w/apples, cinnamon	6.1	2.7	n.a.	.7	.1	n.a.	n.a.
Puffed Wheat, plain	7.0	4.25	7.9	1.2	.16	.065	2.2
Fortified Cereals							
Life	3.8	5.1	75.0	1.5	1.0	1.2	10.0
Fortified Oat Flakes	4.3	5.1	43.0	20.0	.33	.40	3.33
Total	4.6	2.5	n.a.	10.0	1.0	1.24	10.0
Team	4.6	1.7	n.a.	1.5	.15	n.a.	2.0
Product 19	4.8	2.4	75.0	10.0	1.0	1.2	10.0
Special K	5.0	5.7	n.a.	3.3	.33	.39	3.3
King Vitaman	5.9	n.a.	n.a.	10.0	1.0	1.2	10.0
Kaboom	6.1	n.a.	n.a.	10.0	1.0	1.2	10.0
Wheat Germ	4.1	8.9	n.a.	2.5	.5	.22	1.4
Wheat Germ w/sugar							
'n honey	4.7	6.7	n.a.	1.8	.37	.16	1.0

* Protein value is expresed in grams; other nutrients, in milligrams.
** Serving is approximately 1 ounce as purchased except for egg (2 ounces); muffin (1.7 ounces); milk (4 ounces) and others as indicated in list.
n.a.: data not available.

Reprinted from *The Great American Food Hoax*, copyright 1971 by Sidney Margolius, with permission from the publisher, Walker & Co., Inc.

So, on to the frozen foods, another example of "techno-creativity." Basically, the idea of freezing excess fresh produce for later use is a boon to health. The possibility of bringing foods to areas where they are unavailable fresh is an important dimension to the modern diet. It is also an advantage for people at home who cook in quantities or in advance and wish to use freezing as a way of preserving. But, alas, the frozen food section of most markets is a good two-thirds full of nonfoods. Unbelievably simple meals—dishes and single items, such as macaroni and cheese or French toast, or desserts—are packaged attractively to trap the contemporary consumer. In spite of the preservative nature of freezing, chemical additives are added to a large number of frozen foods. In addition, consumer studies have found that the transporting conditions for frozen foods are inadequate, in many cases subjecting the foods to spoilage.

Personally, I feel that the most outrageous infringements committed by the frozen food industry are the packages of frozen vegetables with a little extra sauce and/or spices. The price compared to the plain frozen vegetable is so inflated that the consumer is truly victimized. In my market, plain frozen vegetables are often priced at five packages for eighty-nine cents, whereas a seven-ounce package of frozen peas with potatoes and mushrooms costs forty-nine cents. A 2½-pound bag of frozen mixed vegetables is sixty-nine cents, but an eight-ounce package of mixed vegetables in onion sauce is forty-seven cents. Surely the budget-minded customer must shop this section carefully. And always the store's own brand will be cheaper than a nationally known product.

Over the years, the popularity of frozen vegetables has cut into the canned food industry. A recent consumer study has shown that the drained weight of canned fruits and vegetables is much less than the net weight claimed on the can. Furthermore, an appreciable percentage of the samples (liquid and all) weighed less than the total weight-of-contents specification on their labels. Certainly the canned food area is one in which the shopper should try to buy only on special, though even these products fluctuate so much in price that a bargain may not be a bargain after all. Consequently, canned foods are one of the major targets for truth-in-labeling legislation.

Canned and bottled juices have been under criticism by the natural food advocates for some time. The labeling of many of these is incomplete, because the content of preservatives and antifoaming agents is not indicated on the bottles or cans. And, unless specified to the contrary, most juices contain added sugars. (It's hard to understand why corn syrup need be added to something as naturally sweet as peach nectar.) Then, too, the last few years have introduced the "juice drink," which consists of sugar, water, juice, juice concen-

151

trates, and citric acid. The various percentages are not stated on the label, but the difference in price from pure juice makes me think it is mostly sugar water and flavoring. Again, here is the place to watch for specials and to buy only the real stuff.

Since you may be getting a bit winded and discouraged at this point in our supermarket tour, let me emphasize a general concept. The commitment to good sensible eating can be made in the supermarket, but the decision to do a little simple cooking will have to be made by the careful consumer. Once you learn to avoid the chemical-laden nonfoods, and once you enjoy breezing through the supermarket – confidently buying the basics with ease and expertise and paying careful attention to price discrepancies – you may find you have more money to spare and a lot less tinfoil and packaging materials in the trash can.

Now we come to the meat section. I shop only in supermarkets where there are butcher shops. The countless studies done by both zealots and moderates on packaged meats have turned me off the packaged-meat counters. True, in a butcher shop, too, you can get watered, substandard meat laced with chemicals and extenders, but the chances for better buys and better quality are definitely with a substantial meat department that smells and looks clean and has a minimal turnover in butchers. And if you get acquainted with the butcher you can request skillful trimming and total viewing of the cut you buy. A good butcher will take pride in satisfying personal tastes and desires of his customer. If you have a freezer, or even a good cold refrigerator, you can make a worthwhile saving by buying on special, but remember to ask questions about any new cuts that may cost considerably more than the familiar pieces.

Most of the old stand-by cookbooks have good advice on how to select meat. Considering rising meat costs, you should pay for the weight of a bone only if you are going to: (1) cut it off for soup or beans, or (2) braise (brown and steam) the meat, in which case the bone will add flavor. Don't select meat with excessive fat unless you plan to use the fat. Unless your family consumes all the parts of the

152

chicken, you may be wise to buy only the parts you prefer. You can, however, use the back, wings, and neck for soup stock, and then it is a little cheaper to buy the whole chicken and cut it up yourself. There is no question that fresh fish is better than canned or frozen pieces, but its availability is a geographical privilege. If you are using frozen fish, do not let it sit after it is thawed or the natural moisture will run out quickly and the fish will become tasteless. It's best to cook it slightly frozen. Remember that the prepared meat loaves and patties include the labor of preparation in the pound pricing. And do not pay for the fancy packaged-meat extenders. Oatmeal, wheat germ, or any cooked grain will be better for you and far cheaper. Add your own spices and herbs.

153

The produce section is fun for the Californian since the choices are good all year long. Throughout my travels around the country last year in the early spring, I was amazed to see so much fresh produce in areas still covered with snow. And we are seeing more and more organically grown produce in regular supermarkets, though it is best to check with your grocer on the sources of these fruits and vegetables since they are still considerably more expensive, unless the source is nearby and the item is in season. If you are concerned about pesticides, it is a good idea to buy produce with thick skins that can be peeled, and to wash well and/or peel any nonorganic produce. Though much of the nutritional value is in the outer skin of the fruit or vegetable, the problem of pesticide accumulation is real. Talk to your grocer about looking for reputable organic sources. I have discovered that most produce salesclerks really eat vegetables and fruits and do know something about buying and preparing foods. Happily, organically grown root vegetables are becoming more available at reasonable prices because they can be stored and shipped without too much danger of spoilage.

Here are a few tips for selecting produce. Head lettuce still appears to have the best taste and texture of the commercially grown lettuces, though this may vary with geographical location. Since all lettuces run very high from time to time, try substituting cabbages, red and green, in your salads. They also run high frequently, but there is more volume for the money. Break away from the simple green salad when lettuce is expensive and grate root vegetables and summer squashes. When buying onions for salads, use scallions (green onions) and the sweet red variety. Yellow and white onions are much stronger and should be used for cooking. Use heavy-skinned potatoes for baking and the thinner skins for boiling and mashing. Their prices can dictate your menu. When avocados are purchased hard, they can be ripened by putting them into paper bags for two to three days or until soft. Bananas are a matter of taste. The greener they are, the more starch they contain, while the riper, darker bananas are higher in sugar content. As a rule of thumb, citrus fruits should be selected for their smooth, shiny skins. The coarser, duller skins will contain drier, pithier fruit. Buy firm white mushrooms with nonwithered, well-fluted skirts.

Leaving the produce section, we can stop briefly to count the varieties of bottled salad dressings. Somehow these shelves strike me as the most tragicomic example of culinary laziness. There are sixty different bottles in my market, nearly all containing some preservative, and all are possible to make at home for a fraction of their bottled cost. This section is a first cousin to nondairy creamers and instant puddings. Even the most modestly trained cook can put together a good salad dressing. So, move to the next aisle and select a good salad oil without preservatives (avoid those containing cottonseed oil as the plants are highly sprayed). Find a nice wine vinegar. Toss the salad lightly with a few drops of oil, add salt and

pepper, and toss with a little vinegar. Add some good French mustard and some fresh garlic and you are an expert.

I would like to insert a few words about two controversial subjects, pet food and baby food. Consumer studies indicate that dry pet foods are the most nutritious as well as the most economical, although nine out of ten readers will say that their pets will absolutely *not* eat that "dry stuff." Moreover, they will only eat the most expensive tinned foods. What can I suggest except that you have a long talk with your animal about inflation and the value of foraging for itself?

Baby food is a more serious consideration. Consumer research has found many flaws in prepared baby foods, from excessive water content and low nutritional value to an excessive use of additives. That should be enough to convince the consumer that mashing fresh food in a blender is the best way to feed the small child of the modern world. Frankly, I think that the pallid texture of these canned baby foods is the prelude to many bad eating habits among American children and young people.

The ready-baked goods section is the last one worth considering in my market. Fortunately, the selection of decent breads is increasing and it is possible to find good whole-grain breads without preservatives in most supermarkets today. Learn to be a good label reader in this area, and don't bother to watch for specials. Unless your market has a good day-old counter where bargains are real, breads on special are usually the plastic varieties, and the overcarbohydrated American can well afford to be selective here. Should you buy cookies and crackers, the same principle of careful label reading is necessary.

As we leave the supermarket exhausted, but, I hope, slightly more conscious of today's food empire, I implore you to ignore the ice-cream section for the time being. Much has been said recently about the contents of commercial ice cream, some of which would leave your head spinning. At your local library, check the August 1972 issue of *Consumer Report* and read the ice-cream story.

To be sure, even the most careful shopper in today's supermarket will find it impossible to create an ideally pure diet, for nearly every food on sale has been tampered with to some degree. But, for most Americans, there are few alternatives, and so the only sensible solution is to become a more discriminating, less vulnerable shopper. Buy specials without succumbing to other unnecessary purchases that day. Buy the cheaper house brands, as there is little if any difference between them and the big-name brands. Read labels carefully and select foods containing a minimum of processing and chemical adulteration. Above all, don't buy any more nonfoods. As the awareness of our food folly increases, stricter laws and regulations requiring complete labeling and limiting, if not eliminating, of harmful chemicals will certainly be imposed on the manufacturers. Ultimately the burden of proof lies with the government, but until then the responsibility is on the consumer.

ADDITIONAL READING

Cadwallader, Sharon, and Ohr, Judi. *Whole Earth Cook Book*. Boston: San Francisco Book Company/Houghton Mifflin Company.

Consumer Product Information (United States Government Pamphlet). Washington, D.C.: Consumer Product Information Center.

Cross, Jennifer. *The Supermarket Trap*. New York: Berkley Publishing Corporation.

Goldbeck, David, and Goldberg, Nikki. *The Supermarket Handbook*. New York: Harper & Row, Publishers, Inc.

NOTE:

As this book goes to press, the average prices of many items mentioned in this chapter are rising considerably. This is *more* reason for improving our consumer know-how.

CHAPTER 8

To Honor Our Natural Environment

For the most vital question, in the end, is

not simply how many stomachs the earth can feed,

but how mankind is going to live—the quality of life.

ROLF EDBERG, *On the Shred of a Cloud*

The Question of Land Use

Today as I sit at my typewriter looking out over the Pacific Ocean watching the sun gather the colors of late afternoon, I wonder about the permanence of this vision. How long before this horizon is highrise and my small house is replaced by a condominium?

A friend of mine once said, "The law of ownership is the ability to use well." I have thought many times that that simple statement could be a valuable guide to taking care of our nation's lands if we could agree upon a definition of what it means "to use well." If we take time to review the history of land usage in California, we find that it was originally a source of subsistence, first for the Indians, and then for the Spanish missionaries, who developed the land within the mission walls into small, self-sufficient agrarian communities. Later, when the Mexican government reapportioned these areas, they were awarded as giant land grants to large patrician families. These empires became cattle ranches and private wildlife reserves, and were treated with an attitude that was entirely different from today's. The *patrón* solemnized his acquisition in the presence of a witness by walking about the land, tearing twigs and scattering grass and dirt. He was required to stake out in a hand-drawn map the boundaries of the area for which, and to which, he was responsible. He was obligated to build *and* occupy a house on that land within a year.

161

In Celebration of Small Things

This reverence for one's personal land did not survive the Yankee rush into California. The nineteenth century altered the evaluation of land from an appreciation of its physical beauty and resources into the recognition of the space as money. People began to buy, sell, and lease their land for profit. Few cared if it was divided into lots and sold again, or if numbers of houses were erected at the expense of the natural terrain and the flora and fauna. The practice of land speculation existed well over a hundred years ago in California, and lumbering started as early as 1840. The difference is that now speculation is done by big companies with and for tax write-offs.

Of course, not all the land was disposed of recklessly, since much of it continued to be well used as farmland. Today, the central valley of California is still farming area, but the style of farming has altered. The small farmer, once a proud and vital part of our nation, can no longer resist the change. Watching the development of land around him and suffering from the resulting rise in taxes on his property, he is eventually forced to sell to the real estate developers or the large corporate farms with their elaborate machinery, poorly paid workers, and tax loopholes. More often than not, he capitulates to the times, sells his property, and retires to the city or to a small plot of his original land. It is estimated now that 60% of all farmland in the country is corporately owned.

True, we cannot deny the increase in population and the corresponding need for housing, but we have evolved into a society in which the building of houses is rarely left up to the occupant. Huge corporations are responsible for booming housing developments. And often these corporations are simply major industrial companies looking for a place to invest profits and create tax shelters. Motivated by profit, they care little about the land on which they are building or the durability of the structures. Since expediency and low cost are the controlling factors, most of the building is done on flat land or rolling hills formerly used for farming. Land is money, and land-money has become a major business investment in our generation. Even the most judicious citizen today has difficulty not visualizing at least a

162

slight profit in the value of his land as the years pass. "Landvalue" has become one word to the modern American. "Value for what?" asked the naturalist Joseph Wood Krutch. The tragic irony to which we have been blinded is that it is the cost that rises and not the value. The timeless value of land with pure air, space, and beauty decreases as its value in money rises.

Finally, crowning this century's abuse and misunderstanding of land usage is the government's battle against the conservationist minority's attempts to hold on to public lands. Only one-third of the nation's land is publicly owned. It is not enough that we sell beautiful acreage for speculative housing and plastic recreational development: we now have the problem of trying to maintain what remains of the public lands for the preservation of wildlife and natural forces, in the face of recurring legislative attempts to make them available for mining, lumber, big ranching, and real estate.

This indiscriminate push toward development in the last thirty years has made it difficult for the few conservation-oriented Congressional representatives to battle those projects financed by private interests. A supreme example of the irresponsible government support of big business is the massive power plant plan for the Colorado plateau. The entire Southwest is affected by this grid, which will be the largest fossil-fueled, power-generating complex in the world. Beyond the two plants already operating—one in New Mexico and the other in southwestern Nevada—four others are planned: two in Utah, one in Arizona, and one more in New Mexico. All will be fueled by coal, obtained mostly from strip mining in the area. Three of the proposed four are under construction. The power from the plants will be carried by giant transmitting lines across the desert to urban Southern California, Las Vegas, Phoenix, and Tucson. Besides the effect on the landscape, visualize the growth in population in those urban centers.

Anyone who has witnessed the scarred topography from strip mining in other areas of the country can imagine what the picture will be in the Southwest, one of the most beautiful regions left in the

163

United States. Probably the greatest single sorrow in this master plan is that the area deeply affected is the Black Mesa, the traditional sacred earth of the Hopi and Navaho. The coal for the two existing plants is stripped from this high plateau, and by 1976 another plant will pull from the Black Mesa. In addition, the water to slurry the coal is pumped from the deep natural reserves of the Indians, who fear pollution and depletion of their precious resource. What is even

more alarming is that the varied topography in the Southwest is extremely vulnerable to air pollution since cool air tends to compress the lower layer of warm air for days, preventing any movement. The amount of smoke-pollution emission from these plants is such that the skies may forever be darkened in that part of the country. Already the Four Corners Plant in New Mexico is considered to be the single worst air polluter in the nation. Even if company management observes all regulations and standards for pollution control, there will be little effect on the tons of noxious smoke to be anticipated in the next few years. And the attitude of power companies about their pollution is hardly exemplary, considering they put eight times more money and energy into advertising than into general research, which includes the pollution-control studies too.

For a country whose brains and talent have designed unequaled technological systems, a reorganization of land use and ownership should not be difficult. What, then, can we do to stop this wanton abuse of the earth of America? The answer, of course, is for all individuals to refuse to involve themselves in any business venture that jeopardizes the nation's lands for people, plants, and the animals, now and forever. "To use well" is simply that. Unfortunately, the transition to that sort of thinking will be slow for us after years of moving in a different direction. Therefore, to give us a kick down the road to survival, environmentalists have spelled out the following legislative moves:

1. Make public the conditions set forth in the 1902 Reclamation Act that state that no one shall be entitled to Federal irrigation water for more than 160 acres, and that the recipient be a legitimate farmer-resident. Furthermore, legislation should be created to establish acreage limitations, especially in areas where the ecostructure is in immediate jeopardy.

2. Adopt and support the Family Farm Act, which eliminates big conglomerates from farming.

3. Support the request for higher wages and better working conditions for all farm laborers.

4. Redirect the agricultural colleges' curricula toward assisting the small farmers and co-operatives and to divert their research away from the petrochemical industry and into areas of natural, organic farming methods.

5. Agitate for and support honest distribution of railroad lands to small farming and conservation.

6. Design and promote proper control for land use and zoning laws on local levels with stringent fines for abuse by land developers.

7. Promote the public purchase of scenic areas around towns and cities.

8. Update existing legislation, especially the Homestead Act, whereby the Federal government purchases rural land, reduces the price, and makes it available to the small farmer or co-operative.

9. Eliminate the underassessment of big landowners by promoting state legislation (to apply to anyone, individual or corporation) that increases the tax rate with the more land he, she, or they acquire.

10. Cut earned profits from land held by large corporations by eliminating the tax loopholes of capital gains, accelerated depreciation, and tax loss farming.

11. Restore the original purpose of the crop subsidy program, which was to keep the small farmer on the land and to raise the prices of his produce by paying him not to work certain acreage. Such subsidies should *not* be extended to the big landowner, who is reaping the benefits of this legislation now.

12. Establish rural land trusts to preserve forest lands and to insure that benefits from tourism and public recreation go directly to local areas.

13. Impose strict legislation on all governmental levels to inhibit the expansion of strip mining. This should include a supporting law to require a removal tax to be used to return the land to something approaching a natural condition.

What Price Power?

The Atomic Energy Commission has expressed its intention to license six hundred to one thousand nuclear power installations in the United States by the end of the twentieth century. All of these plants would be dependent on radioactive material.

With the amount of controversy surrounding the construction of nuclear power plants, my question is this: Who is in favor of nuclear energy? If we are to read any publication espousing environmental opinions, or speak with any scientist with conservationist values, we will find an unequivocal *no* to the building of nuclear reactors as an energy source at this time. Even Dr. Edward Teller, *not* considered to be a dove on the issue of nuclear weaponry, has said, "In my opinion, nuclear reactors do not belong on the surface of the earth." He maintains that construction of such reactors should take place only "deeply underground." Furthermore, Dr. Teller warns that a nuclear bomb "is a relatively safe instrument," compared with a nuclear power plant which produces as much long-lived radioactivity in one year as a thousand Hiroshima bombs. These are strong words for the "bomb father."

In researching the issue of nuclear power, I have been amazed to find that the statistics on the chances of grave problems resulting from the construction and use of the plants vary from expert to expert, but they are all so deep within the danger range that any disagreements and differences seem incidental. The first step, one would assume, is to admit the danger publicly. I daresay that if a proposition for converting to nuclear energy appeared on a national ballot, with present risks and advantages carefully listed, the majority would have little question about how to vote. Granted, the criticism of scientific issues and operations requires expertise, but a thorough understanding of the workings and hazards is a big order for the layman. Therefore, considering the gravity of the potential danger of nuclear accidents, the general public has a right to the following: (1) more objective education available in wide-circulation media (i.e., television, newspapers, slick magazines) instead of scientific journals, intellectual publications, and counterculture literature; (2) the assurance that the powerful atomic arm of the government is studying the situation objectively and making recommendations based solely on the advantages and dangers of nuclear energy.

Nuclear Reactors

The primary risks of the common lightwater reactor at this point are these: (a) effluents and fallout resulting from the routine operation of a power plant; (b) insufficient plans for the routine disposal

167

of routine wastes (the nuclear power plant located at Humboldt Bay in Eureka, California, has had continual complaints from employees of dangerous contamination over the last ten years, and in 1973 the national press covered the leakage of more than 100,000 gallons of radioactive wastes from the Atomic Energy Commission facility in Hanford, Washington); (c) problems with the water pipes that conduct the heated water away from the core of the reactors; (d) problems with the emergency core coolants systems designed to bring aid in cases of heating problems; and (e) inadequate emergency procedures for the surrounding population in the event of an accident in the plant. In short, (a) and (b) are routine problems that exist now and have not yet been dealt with adequately, and (c), (d), and (e) are possibilities of danger not at all remote. Fact-finding committees, some associated with the Atomic Energy Commission and some not, have admitted and substantiated the existence of these problems; this testimony itself is no small index, considering the potential catastrophic effect of any one of them.

Another problem with the growing nuclear economy is what we will do with spent fuel elements from the breeder reactors, the second generation of nuclear reactors. Since warnings of the imminent depletion of the high-grade uranium ore that is used to fuel lightwater reactors, the nuclear-industrial marriage has brought forth a reactor which would utilize a lower-grade fuel, producing more waste than from the previous reactor. Nuclear fuel is not trivial waste. At the time of this writing there is only one reprocessing plant in the country (although two new plants are planned). Therefore, all the used fuel elements picked up from plant to plant are transferred to New York for processing. The transportation of the fuel demands perfect conditions to avoid any accidents or contamination. Furthermore, the Atomic Energy Commission's Dr. John Goffman has said that the proposed plant in South Carolina is expected to handle the processing of fuel elements from fifty or so large nuclear power plants. And because the plant stores its radioactive wastes for at least five years, the inventory will grow to

3850 megatons of nuclear material. This, in terms of long-lived radioactivity, is equivalent to 192,000 Nagasaki atom bombs. The transfer, storage, or disposal of wastes and spent fuel—not only of nuclear power plants, but also of the 101 nuclear-powered submarines, five surface ships, and the hundred or so small reactors belonging to the Atomic Energy Commission and various private and university laboratories throughout the country—demand immediate attention. Furthermore, some contracts for reactors that we have built for foreign countries stipulate that the by-products be shipped back to the United States for disposal. If we think we have a garbage problem now . . .

Another matter of concern in the maintenance of nuclear power plants is the efficiency of low-level disposal routines. An adequate dumping procedure for contaminated rags, clothing, tools, instruments, and miscellaneous items is essential. They too will have to be hauled off to disposal sites. With all this need for extraordinary transportation systems, the United States Department of Transportation, responsible for shipping all nuclear material, is grossly understaffed and complains that it cannot cope with the safety procedures necessary.

If only the A.E.C. could recognize that its two basic functions—the promotion of nuclear energy for peace, and the regulation and control of nuclear power plants—have become a conflict of interest. The second responsibility should be relegated to something like the Environmental Protection Agency, especially in view of the lack of adequate legislation to insure the populace that these utility companies would assume full and complete liability in the event of an accident. Surely with even this brief review of the problems related to the use of nuclear energy we should recognize that it is not a safe source of power in its present state of development (or lack of it).

What, then, are the alternatives to nuclear power? We have already discussed the tragedies evolving from the strip mining for coal which has so far been the primary fuel for our power plants. And we are constantly reminded of the cost of piping natural gas, and the problems of oil rights, and the pollution problems caused by transporting and burning both fuels, not to mention the depletion of the sources. What are some of the possibilities for future energy?

Less developed options are: (1) tidal power, (2) cultivation of high-energy algae for conversion to methane, for direct power plant conversion, or for direct power plant combustion, or (3) the production of low-sulphate oil from garbage, animal waste, and coal. But probably the two most talked-about alternate energy sources are geothermal and solar energy.

Geothermal Power

Also known as magma power, geothermal energy comes from water heated by molten rock many thousands of feet beneath the earth's surface. Until now, installations of this type have been restricted to locations where underground reservoirs of heated water exist naturally, and the only installation of this sort in the United States is maintained by the Pacific Gas and Electric Company in the geyser area north of San Francisco. However, scientists estimate that the geothermal wells under the Imperial Valley in California could produce two-thirds of California's electrical needs for many years to come. Many countries have had successful, though limited, results with geothermal power: Mexico, Italy, New Zealand, and, of course, Iceland, which enjoys the great natural privilege of being one of the earth's youngest land masses and is literally steaming. In Iceland, geysers and scalding springs are common landmarks, and the inhabitants have truly succeeded in putting the cleanest, largest source of power to work. They have also used this geothermal energy to produce great quantities of food in naturally heated greenhouses.

Scientists at Los Alamos Laboratories in New Mexico think that they are finding a way to expand the potential by drilling into hot, dry underground regions, pumping in cold water, and letting the earth heat the water. They maintain that sufficient boiling water and resultant steam could be produced to drive turbines in a plant above.

170

If their theory is correct, geothermal energy plants could be built anywhere that hot dry rock is available within 25,000 feet of the earth's surface. These scientists also explain that the difference between the temperature of the water which is inserted and that which is withdrawn would be sufficient to maintain circulation by natural convection. Additional pumping would not be a great consideration, so that the cost of such an operation would be lower than the budgets used to erect and maintain the conventional fossil-fuel and nuclear energy plants. Also, as the heat is removed from the rocks, it would cause them to shrink and crack, and it is assumed that this would thus expand the capacity of the operation.

So far the calculations and plans for the dry rock source are based upon models of the projected installations. Research is being conducted to determine whether the cracking of the underground rock could precipitate earthquakes or whether the eventual depletion of existing wells would have any adverse effects on the stability of the earth's surface above. Another possibility is that minerals withdrawn with the heated water might cause corrosion in the machinery. But if further research uncovers no serious drawbacks, we might have at least some of our power needs answered, and cleanly.

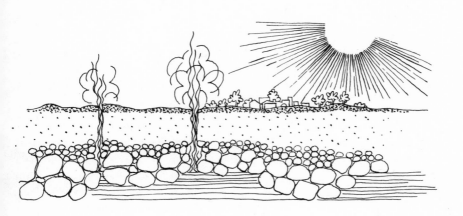

171

Solar Power

Another widely discussed power source is solar energy. Additional research may reveal this to be a significant option indeed. The National Science Foundation has said that solar power technology could satisfy all this country's projected energy requirement, electrical and nonelectrical. Although the techniques for widespread harnessing of this resource are underdeveloped so far, it is not a new concept. Solar-driven pumps and heat engines were built and operated in the United States and abroad from 1870 until just before the First World War.

The potential advantages of solar energy are most impressive. Dr. Jerome Weingart, Senior Research Fellow at the California Institute of Technology's Environmental Quality Laboratory in Pasadena, an expert in the field of solar energy technologies, has claimed:

A solar energy system with an overall operating efficiency of 20% operating in the spring in the southwest part of the country could provide the equivalent of the total U.S. electrical output using an area of less than 4,000 square miles.

To equal the maximum output of the horrendous Four Corners Plant mentioned before, a solar electric plant would need 10% of the incident power of electricity in not more than 40 square miles of land. Even more attractive are the possibilities of separate solar energy converters built into and on private homes. These systems would be considered fuel savers, to be used when supplementary fuel sources were needed for heating systems. The need would vary in different parts of the country. Dr. Weingart says:

In order for solar energy technologies to find widespread household application, it is possible that the major utilities will go into the business of leasing gas and electrically supplemented solar water heating and space conditioning appliances as part of what is already a capital intensive business—to supply a basic energy service. If just four percent of the housing units in Southern California were converted each year to solar water heating/space conditioning, and each solar unit provided 75% of the heat normally supplied by gas and electricity, this would offset the related energy demand due to mushrooming construction. If, over a three-decade period, two-thirds of the residential units in the United States were provided with such solar equipment, more energy would be saved each year than is currently produced by all of the electrical power plants in the U.S.

The most fascinating projection is the possibility of converting incident sunlight in space into microwave energy by using a satellite system. The microwaves would be beamed back to earth, collected, and converted to electrical energy. To catch a sunbeam—such is the poetry of science.

At present, however, the amount of space and capital investment required to harness and store solar energy has been a prohibitive rationale for not instituting more research in this area. But if a definite need for this type of power were ever actually established, we can be sure that our technological genius could eliminate the obstacles very quickly. Geothermal and solar power would not only furnish us with a clean energy source, but could eliminate the international competition over fossil fuel as well.

Certainly we cannot deny the need for continued research in these areas. They are still great dreams, but considering the many serious shortcomings of nuclear power, we must begin to actualize the dreams. Perhaps the solution to our future needs will be a combination of energy sources. Perhaps what this country needs is not an Atomic Energy Commission but an *energy commission*, controlled by Congress and dedicated to funding research into all forms of energy. But what is needed immediately is a change of attitude regarding power. We have become so helplessly dependent on an "unlimited everything" that all this recent talk about an energy squeeze seems to most people to be no more than the boy who cried, "Wolf." The truth, however, is that as more and more energy-demanding gadgets appear on the market, utility bills will rise, and the crunch will be more than just talk. Consequently, the utility companies' argument for installing nuclear power plants will gain more popularity. It would seem that the best way to protect ourselves from high cost as well as pollution is to start now to institute a slow and sustained cutback in the day-to-day demands in our houses and businesses. The commitment to such activity must be in the form of a new consciousness, which requires a good deal of reminding oneself in the beginning, but like everything else, it will eventually become a habit, and a good one.

Obtaining a little background information about power helps a layman to put the crisis into perspective. Gas is generally cheaper than electricity if natural gas is available where you live. A gas water heater, for instance, is less than half the cost of an electric heater to maintain. Installation is more costly for gas if the pipeline is not near the location of the heater, but if you have a natural gas line, it pays in the long run to invest in a gas heater. The rates increase threefold in the Northeast because the natural gas fields are located in the Southwest. The cost of electricity is cheaper in low-cost power regions of the TVA and the Pacific Northwest. Therefore, the price you pay locally per therm or cubic foot of gas versus what you pay locally for a kilowatt of electricity will determine what is cheaper in your house. There is a minimum charge for both gas and electricity, and most often natural gas is cheaper for house heating than oil or electricity, and also it is generally cheaper for major appliances in your house, including air conditioning. The more you use, the cheaper will be the cost per unit. Such is the rationale offered by the utility companies, but always remember that the more electricity you use, the more fossil fuel is consumed.

As is commonly known, electricity is always used to operate motor-driven or electronically powered items such as televisions, radios, and phonographs. In the past, electricity was generally used only for these items while gas was generally used to fuel heat-producing items, like stoves, central heating, and water heaters, although there were exceptions like gas refrigerators, gas clothes dryers, and electric heaters. Now electricity is used exclusively in many homes. At this writing, the more items you have that draw the same type of power, the lower your monthly bill will be, as block

174

rates are cheaper. If you live in an area where the electricity costs less than one cent per kilowatt-hour, it is cheaper to run your house on electricity. Also, many electric companies are offering special low rates if you use electric heat or install an electric water heater. If you are planning to buy or build a new house, you would be well advised to look into the local utility company's rates before choosing your heating system. The thing to remember, however, is that because of the increasing crisis over energy sources, we are not certain what comparative costs for power will be in the future. This is all the more reason to work toward lowering your general power consumption.

The United States, which constitutes 6% of the world's population, uses 35% of the world's present energy output. Although the primary power wolf is still industry, it stands to reason that all effort to cut back power is a contribution to reducing that figure. For those who are interested in incorporating power conservation into their own everyday living, some suggestions on cutting down waste and pollution follow.

Electric Lighting

1. Avoid using electricity during the day by opening blinds and curtains to utilize all natural light.

2. Use sufficient, but not excessive, wattage. Keep lights on only in the area you are using.

3. Keep all light fixtures clean to insure maximum lighting.

4. Remember to turn off outside, garage, and cellar lights. Don't let your paranoia lead you to leaving porch lights on all night. It is unlikely to deter crime.

Heat

1. Check the chart on page 177 and try to reduce the big power drains. Heating and air conditioning are the culprits, and during cold weather it is much wiser and healthier to get in the habit of wearing more clothes and lowering the heat. Once you have become

accustomed to this, you will find your energy level increases and you are not as prone to temperature-change colds.

2. Except in zero-weather areas, keep the heat off at night. Use more blankets and you will find you sleep better.

3. Avoid drawing too much electricity at peak load times. Keep the heat or air conditioning on very low all day even when you are gone, as turning on full power in the evening simply adds to the big draw. Of course, make sure your heating arrangement has a thermostat and is safe.

4. Check your heater to see if it has a filter, and, if so, change it frequently. Vacuum the bottom of a wall heater to prevent possible hazards from dust clogging. This saves money by reducing malfunctioning and fire damage.

5. Keep air registers and returns free of obstruction to allow air to get back to the furnace, or heat will not be distributed where you need it.

6. Keep the thermostat clean and consistently set. If it is clean, you will avoid faulty readings and settings, and a consistent temperature will help eliminate high costs from overcompensating settings.

7. Caulking, weather stripping, and insulation will greatly reduce your heat bills and cut down on waste heat.

8. Keep draperies and curtains closed at night to keep out cold and hold in heat.

9. Close registers and shut off radiators in rooms not frequently used.

10. Close the damper in the fireplace when you are not using it so that neither heated nor cooled air will escape.

Appliances

1. Use your dishwasher, washing machine, and clothes dryer only for full loads. You'll save water and electricity.

2. Don't overdry your clothes. It's hard on them and your utility bill.

3. Keep the lint filter clean in a clothes dryer. Your dryer will operate more efficiently in less time.

4. Set the water heater at the highest temperature your hands can stand and no hotter, for the cold water needed to cool the water wastes the heat that was needed for the hot water. Washing clothes with too-hot water is hard on them anyway.

5. When building, either locate the water heater near the kitchen and bathroom to reduce hot-water-pipe heat losses, or if it must be at a distance because of gas piping, insulate the pipes leading to the faucets if they are accessible and exposed.

6. Never put any heat-producing appliance on the refrigerator or the refrigerator close to the water heater, as a refrigerator has to work harder in heated areas.

7. Don't allow frost to build up in the freezer. It makes the refrigerator work harder.

8. Don't overheat the oven, and always keep the broiler door closed. If you invest in a new oven, get one with a window, because frequent peeking uses extra fuel.

9. Use tight-fitting lids on pots and pans to keep in steam and reduce cooking time.

10. Don't leave an appliance on after you have finished using it. It's safer, cheaper, and less polluting. Do not leave the radio and television on to entertain the atmosphere. Invest in natural sounds. Furthermore, eliminate any appliance not absolutely necessary to your life style (I hope a conservative one). Beware of silly electrical gadgets (see Chapter 1).

Appliance	Average Wattage	Estimated Use Per Day	Annual KWH Consumed	Average Monthly Cost
Heat Pump (Combined air conditioner and heater)	11,848	3.7 hr.	16,003	15.00
Water Heater (Quick recovery)	4,474	2.9 hr.	4,811	5.50

Appliance	Average Wattage	Estimated Use Per Day	Annual KWH Consumed	Average Monthly Cost
Water Heater (Standard)	2,474	4.7 hr.	4,219	4.80
Refrigerator (12 cu. ft.)	241	8.2 hr.	728	1.29
Refrigerator-Freezer (Frostless–14 cu. ft.)	615	8.2 hr.	1,829	3.40
Refrigerator-Freezer (14 cu. ft.)	326	9.6 hr.	1,137	2.08
Food Freezer–Frostless (15 cu. ft.)	440	11 hr.	1,761	3.23
Food Freezer (15 cu. ft.)	341	9.6 hr.	1,195	2.15
Air Conditioner	1,566	2.4 hr.	1,389	2.40
Range	12,207	16 min.	1,175	2.22
Clothes Dryer	4,856	34 min.	993	1.85
Television (Black and white)	237	4.2 hr.	362	.66
Television (Color)	332	4.1 hr.	502	.86
Dehumidifier	257	9.6 hr.	377	1.61
Dishwasher	1,201	50 min.	363	.69
House Fan (Medium)	370	2.2 hr.	291	1.31
Roll-about Fan	171	2.2 hr.	138	.60
Roaster	1,333	25 min.	205	.41
Frying Pan	1,196	26 min.	186	.36
Radiant Heater	1,322	22 min.	176	.58
Humidifier	117	3.8 hr.	163	.49
Electric Blanket	177	2.3 hr.	147	.48
Iron	1,008	23 min.	144	.29
Coffee Maker	894	20 min.	106	.19
Washing Machine	512	33 min.	103	.20
Washing Machine (Wringer)	286	44 min.	76	.15
Broiler	1,436	11.3 min.	100	.21
Hot Plate	1,257	12 min.	90	.19
Radio	71	3.3 hr.	86	.17
Deep Fat Fryer	1,448	9 min.	83	.16

Appliance	Average Wattage	Estimated Use Per Day	Annual KWH Consumed	Average Monthly Cost
Vacuum Cleaner	630	10.8 min.	46	.09
Toaster	1.146	5.6 min.	39	.08
Food Disposer	445	11 min.	30	.05
Waffle Iron	1,116	2.4 min.	22	.04
Shaver*	14	3.5 hr.	18	.04
Clock	2	24 hr.	17	.04
Sun Lamp	270	9 min.	16	.04
Food Blender	386	6 min.	15	.04
Hair Dryer	381	6 min.	14	.04
Food Mixer	127	17 min.	13	.04
Sewing Machine	75	24 min.	11	.04
Carving Knife	92	12 min.	8	.02
Toothbrush*	7	1.9 hr.	5	.01

* Cordless units which are plugged in for recharging as needed during nonuse periods.

The Use of Water

Years ago, when I was living in Mexico, there was a terrible drought in the area. For weeks rains had been expected, but nothing happened. Each day the paper announced the number of weeks of water left in the dam. As the water level continued to drop, the water was shut off each afternoon for four or five hours. Most of the village houses had one source of running water, but we had a bathroom too. At first it was an inconvenience, for we could not remember to stash a little cooking water in the morning. But, as time passed, we became accustomed to these dry hours and we all became more conservative about our general water use. Since then I have had an aversion to running water waste. I remember, too, that when we were children my mother objected if we ran water to rinse the dishes or used too much in the bathtub. She had grown up without running water in her house.

179

Water Conservation at Home

1. Check your house for faucet leaks. Drips can be a deceptive and expensive waste of water, and also of heating if the leak is in a hot-water faucet. A running toilet is also a waste of money and water. Watch to see that the water is not dripping into the bowl between flushes. It may mean the water level is too high and this can be remedied by adjusting the arm to a lower level, or it may mean a new seal is needed around the ball.

2. You can displace the water in your toilet tank, and thus use less, if you put a brick or heavy stone in it.

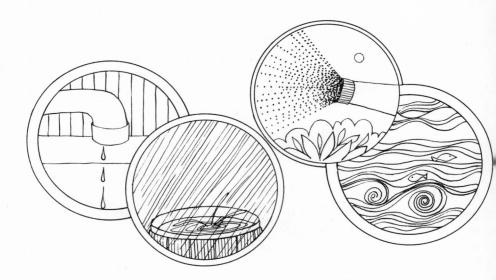

3. Cut down on your showering time. True, it is one of life's great luxuries, but leave some pleasures for your grandchildren. Try turning off the water while lathering and turning it on again to rinse. This also applies to shaving and brushing your teeth.

4. Save excess running water or drainage in spring water tanks, or even cooking water, to water house and garden plants.

5. Do not use the toilet as a waste basket for cigarettes and such

junk. It wastes water in flushing, often clogs the pipes, and adds more pollutants to the environment.

6. Do not water your garden in full sunlight or in the heat of the day. You will waste water in evaporation.

7. If you are ambitious and have a garden, especially in an area where there are dry spells, the old-fashioned rain barrel is a wonderful suggestion. Provided it is tight, the rain barrel is the best way to collect the water that comes out of the spout under the eaves. An average roof can yield up to three hundred barrels a season. If the water is hard in your area, rain water will be a joy for washing your hair.

General Pollution Problems

We have been warned for several years about the giant dump we are creating out of the earth. As a result of increasing air and water pollution, ravage of the land, and the tragicomic image of litter in space, we are faced with some dramatic needs for clean-up, or else. In 1972, the *New York Times* published a story claiming that pollution was also changing our climate. A physical oceanographer with the National Oceanic Atmosphere Administration has reported some interesting (to use that guarded academic term) findings. For instance, the Atlantic Ocean has risen three inches in the last eight years as opposed to four inches per century for the last three thousand years. The water has come from the melting of the polar ice caps of both the Arctic and Antarctic, and, since there is now more water in the ocean, we can look forward to more rain. The absolute conclusion of these findings is not yet available and scientists are not in agreement as to whether the land is receding because of the removal of so much water and petroleum from the earth, or if the waters are rising from the melting of the polar ices, or possibly both. Many environmentalists feel the changes may be due to the releasing of so much carbon dioxide in the atmosphere, which heats up the earth's surface and melts the glaciers. And it is the burning of fossil fuel that creates the carbon dioxide. It is also possible that the

181

amount of smoked particles being put into the upper atmosphere and cutting the sunlight could bring about a dangerous fall in temperatures. Furthermore, the alteration in the ice caps could conceivably affect the rotation of the earth. Such changes make the pollution on my beach fairly insignificant, although certainly important to the immediate residents.

There is no question that we must turn over some new leaves. Every day the paper offers reports on such large-scale projects as the installing of the Alaska pipeline, or the imminent sale of oil and gas leases in the Gulf of Mexico. These occurrences, in the light of the recent terrible oil spills, appear to be more examples of corporate and government irresponsibility.

Furthermore, the FDA has been dragging its feet in the relief of many acute dangers such as drugs and chemicals in foods, pesticides, and phosphates. One issue that deserves consistent attention is the amount of detergents filling our lakes and rivers. After the appearance of biodegradable products in the mid-sixties, we began to see some of the detergent foam disappear from the tops of the waters, but biodegradability is not enough, since the elements into which the biodegradable detergents decompose are equally significant. The effects of even the biodegradable detergents reveal yet another example of industrial society's acceleration of the natural evolutionary processes to cause effects within a period of several decades that would ordinarily occur in the course of thousands of years.

Eutrophication is the process whereby plant life takes precedence over animal life. This has occurred in lakes and rivers where algae are overstimulated by an excess in nutrients and rot and die, using up the oxygen supply in the water. The fish are deprived of the necessary oxygen needed to survive and the plant growth takes over until the accumulating vegetation and decay displace the water and the area dries up. This cycle is occurring in all areas where the key nutrient for the process, phosphorus, is run off. Though phosphorus enters the waters from sources such as soil erosion, animal and plant decay, and sewage, it is estimated that over 50% of the phosphorus entering rivers and lakes is from detergents. Phosphate builders have been used in detergents since the war years and are extremely effective in removing grease and suspending dirt, but the fact is that these phosphates end up in our surface waters to create this cyclic death of our clear lakes and streams. Though the detergent industry refuses to admit that these phosphates contribute to the process of eutrophication, the government is finally beginning to face the danger to our waters posed by detergents, biodegradable or not.

Unfortunately, most Americans have become so dependent on these heavy-duty fabric and dish cleaners that it is difficult to alert the public to the gravity of the problem. The problem of getting stains out of synthetic fabrics is truly a chore without the effect of phosphates. Until the industry comes up with an adequate alternative (and not an alternative killer), the best the consumer can do is to use the lowest-phosphate cleaner available. Where the water is soft or where houses have water softeners, especially near fresh water, low phosphates should definitely be used since part of the effectiveness of high-phosphate detergents is to soften the water. Check the available low-phosphate detergents in your market and experiment with their effectiveness.

In spite of all the talk about pesticides, contamination of the soil, and consumer poisoning, modern agronomy still faces some serious problems. Thousands of acres of good farmland are burning out from years of saturation of chemicals, and yet whole farms are financed by the fertilizer and pesticide business. As a consequence, agribusiness is facing a death grip, and it is truly the petrochemical industry that is fertilizing the farmer. Now, with chemically devastated lands contributing to the declining productivity and higher production costs, the problems of modern farming are mounting. Let us hope, now that young and ambitious biologists are concerned with natural pest controls and are contributing to the research in natural organic farming methods, that viable alternatives will soon be available to the modern farmer who receives more and more demand for organically raised produce.

183

General Pollution Control

The following suggestions are offered for beginning the campaign to eliminate as many high-level pollutants from our everyday lives as possible.

1. Do not wait for the local sewage plants to eliminate phosphates from waste water. We will save on taxes if we begin using low-phosphate cleaning compounds. If you use regular laundry soap for washing clothes, add ¼ cup baking soda to ¾ cup laundry soap. This will help achieve the cleansing effect of detergents.

2. Do not use chemical pesticides in the house. These chemicals live for a long, long time and are very harmful to plants and animals. Avoid the pest-control strips. Return to old-fashioned fly paper or fly swatters. The exercise is good for the sedentary modern American.

3. Not everyone can find room for a compost pile, but if there is a gardener in your area who cultivates a compost heap, save your wet garbage in an airtight container and contribute it a couple of times a week. A garbage-disposal unit is hard on the sewage system.

4. The best biological pest controls are: lady bugs (lady birds, lady beetles, ladybird beetles), praying mantises (they eat other insects), *Trichogramma* (a tiny parasite wasp), *Bacillus thuringiensis* (bacteria), milky spore disease (a fungus for some beetles). For obtaining organic pest controls see the list at the end of the chapter.

5. To dispose of pesticides you have on hand, write to this address for information on how to proceed: Working Group on Pesticides, CS22 Parklawn Building, 5600 Fishers Lane, Rockville, Md. 20852.

6. Observe the problems of noise pollution. Become more sensitive to noises in your immediate environment. Many of them can be eliminated, especially those from such mechanisms as power saws and power mowers.

7. Plan to operate your car in the most efficient manner possible. Of all types of pollution in the air, the automobile emits the highest portion of carbon monoxide and hydrocarbons. At present, a few refineries offer lead-free gasoline. Eventually this will be the only type of automobile fuel available, when cars have been equipped

with catalytic converters that will remove harmful emission. Meanwhile, the following measures will help to cut down on automobile pollution:

a. Maintain clean burning. If you can operate your car on lead-free or low-lead gas, do so. Find what octane rating your car needs and provide the proper fuel. Soon the Federal Trade Commission will require octane ratings on all gas pumps.

b. Check the air cleaner frequently. If air does not get to the engine properly, gas is wasted and more pollution results.

c. Keep your smog-control device or the older crankcase ventilation valves in working order.

d. Keep your tires pumped to their correct pressure to insure efficient movement of your car.

e. Keep your carburetor adjusted correctly. Improper adjustment leads to the release of more hydrocarbons and carbon monoxide.

f. Engine idling wastes gas and adds to air pollution. Don't act like the highway patrol and the school buses.

g. Don't let the gas-station attendant fill your tank too full. (This is commonly called "topping off" the tank.) An overflow results in evaporation of gasoline, which contributes to smog.

h. Recycle your oil if you change it yourself. Try to talk a local gas station into taking it from you.

i. Consider buying a small car. It uses less metal, less space, less gasoline, and less rubber for tires. Since synthetic rubber, made from such polluting agents as natural gas and/or petroleum, nearly equals the amount of natural rubber used, you will be doing smog a worthy disservice by demanding less rubber. It's a vicious cycle because the chemical oxidants in the air attack rubber tires, reduce their life span, and create a need for more rubber.

j. Whenever possible, use public transportation and organize car pools. Diesel buses and electric trolleys emit less carbon monoxide and hydrocarbons than the private auto. Electric trolley systems burn coal which, of course, releases sulphur oxides, but, since they serve many more people than the individual car, they create proportionately less pollution.

185

k. If possible, one family, one car.

Recycling, Part of a Way of Life

Having just received a letter from a friend written on the back of a junk-mail advertisement, I am reminded of the great change that has occurred in the last three to four years in this country in the attitude toward reusable waste. But I am also reminded of the first time I ran across no-deposit bottles many years ago, and I found myself envisioning city dumps filled with giant mounds of bottles. Even at that time there was enough nonreturnable glass to create a problem. Almost anyone who grew up in the forties would be saddened to see future generations deprived of the great American pastime of bottle collecting. Now, however, I and others of my generation are relieved to see the kids of the seventies scrounging the beaches and trash cans for bottles and aluminum cans, even if they are only indirectly cleaning up the environment.

The institution of recycling is here. Cities and towns all over the country are organizing centers to cope with usable items heretofore

relegated to the landscape. In the beginning of this campaign there was not much hope of returning a very high percentage of our production volume, but fortunately Yankee ingenuity is beginning to apply itself. Good news, like the breakthrough in recycling plastic, gives us hope. The Interior Department's Bureau of Mines has reported success with plastic at a Missouri research center in metallurgy. Undifferentiated plastics are cleaned and shredded, and then run through a series of liquids with different specific gravities. In this way the plastics are separated into groups so that they can be treated and reused. Other materials, too, are being successfully recycled. For example, in some recycling centers, nonreturnable glass containers are put into grinders, which help prepare the glass for reuse as well as cutting down on storage problems. Even auto shredders have been developed to recycle automobiles by chewing up the metal in approximately one minute. The metal can then be hauled off to a foundry and cast into usable parts. Sewage sludge, while a dangerous pollutant in its raw form, is being treated, especially in many midwestern areas, and shipped to fertilizer companies.

Some processes of recycling have decided environmental advantages. For instance, melting scrap aluminum to produce secondary aluminum requires a very small energy pull as opposed to the primary process of extracting aluminum from its ore. This is why so many companies are offering to buy back used aluminum beer and pop cans. It is important to recognize all the implications of this recycling process if it is to be carried out to its maximum potential. For example, railroad freight charges were under attack at the end of 1971 by a group of law students in the East because the freight rates had been raised, seriously affecting the shipping of recycled materials. In the summer of 1972, a three-judge Federal court panel ruled that the Interstate Commerce Commission had violated the national environmental laws by failing to do an environmental impact study. Subsequently, the freight rate increase was ordered rolled back. The significance here is that with the level of interest and commitment to recycling among the populace, governmental agencies should certainly exercise all their powers to support these programs or the entire concept of recycling is meaningless.

It is truly encouraging, also, to read that a large market chain in the Midwest, operating in six states, has banned the use of plastic egg cartons, stating that the amount of fossil fuel required to produce these cartons is greater than that required to make paper cartons. Certainly any private industry and business willing to support environmental protective measures should be commended. But if we stop to think about all that remains to be done, we might next ask why the government itself doesn't make the shift to, say, using only recycled paper for all its printing needs instead of paying $14 million for virgin paper as it did in 1972. (See end of chapter for Recycled-Paper Buying Guide.) None of us can afford to minimize any effort to join in the campaign to use what we have used. But more than recycling must be instituted in the national ethic of conservation. Not only should we support all legislation that bans the sale of no-return containers, but we *must* begin to cut back on consumption in general. Let us begin to turn our backs on the Snake-Oil Headquarters on Madison Avenue and develop a sense of prudent consumption. A concerted effort to educate the next generation to accept the ethic of no waste should be an integral part of family, school, and community life.

The time I spent in Mexico was a great experience in the celebration of reuse. I thought I was being very careful, but when my son went to give the wet garbage to the village hogs, the neighbors looked at him as if he were throwing out "la comida."

Very few items in the market were wrapped in paper. All produce was placed in large baskets. Eggs were carried from the vendor in metal baskets. All seeds and legumes and fresh meat were wrapped in scrap paper, and women brought their own jars for foods such as sour cream, shrimp, and oysters. Laundry soap was sold in unwrapped bars. We even had trouble scraping up enough paper to start a fire in the fireplace. Most fascinating to me, though, were the old women vendors who sat on the street corners and roasted pumpkin seeds over a small brazier and sold them as a popular snack, as we do popcorn, only they put them in little cones made out of scrap paper. It was a good world, so free of wrappings and containers and synthetics, but thanks to "hands across the border," supermarkets are beginning to appear, and plastic has become a coveted (and wasted) substance.

One significant way to eliminate waste in your daily life is to set up recycling centers in your community. Post information on preparing items for recycling in public places, and follow these suggestions:

1. Save all metal for reuse. Learn to identify the following:

    a. Aluminum—generally pop-top beer and soda cans, seamless with no bottom lip, very lightweight, not to be confused with the aluminum can with the extruded steel bottom which is tapered and is a newer product (use a magnet if you are unsure).

    b. Bi-metal—also pop-top containers; but they are heavier with a seam along the side with a flat bottom.

    c. Tin—this is actually tinned steel, which is used for pet foods and canned fruits and vegetables. These are the heaviest cans and are recognizable without their labels.

Smash aluminum cans, and remove the ends of the other types, and flatten them. Aerosol cans are not recyclable, so avoid buying them.

2. Try to buy returnable bottles and recycle all other glass, which is sorted by color. Remove foil labels, but you need not bother with the plain paper labels, since the melting-down process will eliminate them. Glass can be reused for containers and can also be used for glass-wool insulation, reflective paint, and to mix with asphalt as a road surface.

3. Return cleaned items only. Residue makes the recycling process messy and unsanitary.

4. Paper and paper items are collected for reuse in some recycling centers. Help organize this process in your community. One ton of recycled paper saves seventeen trees. Reuse paper in your life by:

(a) not using paper bags to bring home groceries, or reusing the bags until they are absolutely exhausted;

(b) using newsprint to clean windows, wrap gifts, and wrap garbage;

(c) using any wax-coated paper from food products to wrap lunch items;

(d) encouraging local businesses not to use paper bags for items purchased;

(e) sharing newspapers and magazines;

(f) not using paper plates and cups. Use fabric towels, napkins, tablecloths, place mats, and diapers. Pretend the paper counterparts do not exist.

5. Plastic recycling is in the early stages, so it is best to avoid buying plastic containers, unless you have some use for them when they are empty.

6. Send old clothing and furniture to be reused to the Goodwill, Salvation Army, and thrift shops. Fortunately, this is the era of "the affinity for old things," so don't dump anything; have a garage sale.

Endangered Wildlife

It is no exaggeration to say that at present many animal and bird species in the United States are gravely endangered, owing in great part to various manifestations of twentieth-century progress. Of those, just a few are listed here:

Eastern Timber Wolf	Sonoran Pronghorn
Red Wolf	Columbian White-tailed Deer
Florida Panther	California Condor
Brown Pelican	Blue Pike
Aleutian Canada Goose	American Alligator
Whooping Crane	Southern Bald Eagle
Ivory-billed Woodpecker	American Peregrine Falcon

190

To protect these, and the many others, there are certain measures that all of us should take at once.

First of all, we should see that commercial products are not made from any animals that have not been raised for commercial purposes. Feathers from most birds have been eliminated from the market for a long time, though a wide variety of fur products is still available. Certain reptiles, such as alligators, are protected by law, but they are still killed and sold by poachers. Consequently, we the consumers must eliminate this market by refusing to buy any item made from these species.

If you must hunt and fish, do so only in season, and observe the set limits. It is fortunate that we have a new generation interested in preserving the disappearing species. I still have a Mother's Day card made by my son when he was in the first grade. On the front is a large banana and inside he had written, "Eat me, but save the wildlife."

This past decade has brought American eco-consciousness out of obscurity and into fashion. The threat to our natural environment has become *the* topic of the time, the crucial issue in the media, politics, and academic curricula. New images and identities have emerged into eco-limelight, and well-known personalities are forced to take eco-stands to maintain their popularity. And while the overemphasis of issues is typical of our society, the problems of pollution, waste, and excessive development are a genuine threat and have been for some time. But so deeply entrenched are our environmental bad habits that it takes an eleventh-hour panic to move us into action. Still, this new energy and promise gives us hope. If we are to remain a technological society and yet not destroy what is left of our natural resources and landscape, we will have to make a major shift in our living patterns within the next few years. What I call "eco-techno-compatibility" does not mean simply a moratorium on the construction of high-rise apartments, or the relocation of a freeway, or the recycling of beer cans. We cannot put the blame on any one aspect of contemporary civilization, be it science, industry, population increase, government, or even capitalism, but neither can any of these forces be exempted. Nor can all the necessary changes be legislated. What is fundamentally necessary is that we regard ourselves as both individual citizens and working members of a societal group, and that we realize we must hold ourselves environmentally accountable on both levels. Only with this acceptance of total responsibility can we create an ethic based on the balance of nature, humankind, and machinery.

ADDITIONAL READING

Barnes, Peter, and Casaling, Larry. *Who Owns the Land* (pamphlet, $ .40). San Francisco: National Coalition for Land Reform, 345 Franklin Street 94102.

Breyerton, G. *Nuclear Dilemma*. New York: Friends of the Earth / Ballantine Books, Inc.

Cloud, P. E. Jr., ed. *Resources and Man*. San Francisco: W. H. Freeman and Company Publishers.

Curtis, R., and Hogan, E. *Perils of the Peaceful Atom*. New York: Ballantine Books, Inc.

Fisher, J. *Wildlife in Danger*. New York: Viking Press.

Goldstein, Jerome. *Garbage As You Like It: A Plan to Stop Pollution by Using Our Nation's Wastes*. Emmaus, Pa.: Rodale Press.

Hightower, James. *Hard Tomatoes, Hard Times*. Cambridge, Mass.: Schenkman Publishing Company, Inc.

National Buyers Guide to Recycled Paper. Washington, D.C.: Environmental Educators, Inc., 1621 Connecticut Ave. N.W. 20009.

Nobile, Philip, and Deedy, John, ed. *The Complete Ecology Fact Book*. New York: Doubleday & Company, Inc.

Recycling. Emmaus, Pa.: Rodale Press Education Series.

Revelle, Roger, and Landsberg, Hans. *America's Changing Environment*. Boston: Beacon Press.

Solar Energy Digest. 7401 Salerno Street, San Diego, Ca. 92111.

Solar Energy Research (pamphlet). Washington, D.C.: United States Government Printing Office.

BIOLOGICAL PEST CONTROL COMPANIES

Bio-Control
Route 2, Box 2397
Auburn, California 95603

Gothard, Inc.
P.O. Box 370
Cantillo, Texas 79835

Thompson-Hayward Chemical Co.
3516 East New York Street
Kansas City, Kansas 66110

Hopkins Agricultural Chemical Co.
P.O. Box 584
Madison, Wisconsin 53701

Vitova Insectory, Inc.
P.O. Box 475
Rialto, California 92835

Fairfield Biological Laboratories
Clinton Corners, New York 12514

Wahco Products Company
6608 San Fernando Road
Glendale, California 91201

NOTE:

The completion of this chapter preceded the current "energy crisis" in the United States and Western Europe. Therefore, many of the warnings and suggestions I have included now have become actualities. It is important to note that while the politics of these shortages has not yet been sorted out, there is no question that there is a limitation of natural resources on this planet. There have been scientific warnings for years that we will eventually run out of fossil fuel because of our industrial expansion and population growth. However, *these realities have been with us a long time* and in no way give us license to expand and reinstitute strip mining or off-shore drilling, or to abuse the environment in any form. Rational answers and solutions lie *only* in developing the alternative *clean* sources of power and an overall *cutback* in our consumption and waste.

CHAPTER 9

Creating a More Cooperative Community

For, by making imaginative use of change to channel change, we cannot only spare ourselves the trauma of future shock, we can reach out and humanize distant tomorrows.

ALVIN TOFFLER, *Future Shock*

UNTIL RECENTLY, the spirit of the cooperative community had seemingly vanished from American life. There are many independent small communities operating throughout the country, but few of them are still interdependent except for a handful of archaic and isolated religious subcultures, which are constantly struggling to stay intact. Over the years, even in the most distant rural communities, the old-fashioned exchange of goods and services has been slowly replaced by the exchange of money and credit cards.

Then, during the middle 1960's, large numbers of young people began to turn their backs on the piercing pace of contemporary living, determining instead to establish new communities and family structures based on a synergistic idea of cooperation and creative energy rather than competition and currency. Though many of these communities have not been able to sustain themselves for all the reasons known to social science, the strength and commitment of these young pioneers have been impressive.

We have seen, in the past few years, many new attitudes toward human interaction. For example, there is now more receptivity to reconstructing and rediscovering living styles of the past in an attempt to regain the great American spirit of sharing work loads and festive rituals. I, for one, do not feel that it is necessary to abandon our homes and present lives to find that sense of community. Rather, I think the potential for it exists wherever there is a cluster of

197

permanent or semi-permanent residents who are interested in making resourceful and creative contact with their neighbors. My own community is a singular example of increasing cohesiveness, and many of the suggestions in this chapter are examples of what is happening in this one small section of the continent's edge.

Undoubtedly you, the reader, will come up with many more ideas than I suggest in the pages that follow; perhaps some of yours will be offshoots of my own, others altogether different. Above all, don't be discouraged by the problems of trying to unite people and reaching agreement on goals and tactics. Encourage everyone to organize his own project, but urge the support of one another's ideas, too. The future is not uniformity or conformity, but a mosaic of contrasting and complementing personalities and lifestyles.

One very effective way to expedite a number of worthwhile additions to community services is to establish a nonprofit corporation to act as overseer of all the projects within its domain. This saves the separate projects, some of which may be very small, from having to go through all the legal business of incorporating and obtaining a nonprofit status.

This type of arrangement was started in our community several years ago and acquired a number of solid and important services needed in the area. The Whole Earth Restaurant (on the University of California campus at Santa Cruz), of which I was a part, is an affiliate of this larger network. Since the other affiliates are not revenue-generating organizations, the original hope was that the restaurant would reroute its profits to these other needy affiliates. However, some affiliates are eligible for special funding—local, state, or federal—and therefore are not able to receive corporation funds. So far, though, there has not been a problem of excess profits, and the most the restaurant has done is to pay back the original loans it accrued in setting up the corporation and the restaurant. But at present this is sufficient, since the restaurant has successfully met the needs of the campus community, and fund-raising projects and special grants have allowed the other affiliates to stay afloat.

The other advantage of the central corporation is that the general accountant of the corporation acts as a financial overseer and adviser and pays the quarterly employee deductions for all the affiliates. Each month the bookkeeper of each separate affiliate turns over the sales tax and the social security, withholding and compensation deductions of its organization to the central accountant. The strength of the center and the duplicate accounting system keep the books straight and up to date. Also, if any affiliate receives a gift of money, it can use the tax exemption status of the nonprofit corporation. Although each affiliate is an independent subdivision, it is subject to the ultimate control and authority of the board of directors of the corporation. Few problems have arisen in this experiment because the basis of the corporation is a philosophical commitment to servicing the community. While there have been no appreciable profits, salaries have been paid and the various affiliates have continued to operate.

The affiliates of this particular corporate venture are these: a day-care center for children of working and student parents, a food co-op, a hardware co-op, a youth hostel, a community switchboard, which is a twenty-four-hour emergency telephone line and question-answering service (I am especially proud of this, for I feel every community needs a distress line), and, most recently, a temporary home for delinquent and predelinquent youth, and a large community garden project. Many similar projects are being developed throughout the country under separate auspices and I am confident the number of community services will increase in the next few years.

Perhaps the most popular of the co-operative movements in the United States and Canada are the organizations set up to buy and sell food. As lamented in Chapter 7, the rising price of food, the misleading advertising, and the consumer's lack of power in determining food needs have laid the foundation for the growing number of co-ops.

There are a number of ways to set up group food stores. Probably the most common is to sell shares of the organization at a minimal price of five or ten dollars. Each member is limited to one vote, regardless of his or her number of shares. Profiteering is eliminated because no dividend is paid on the share capital contributed by the members, although in many instances the initial investment is paid back in goods at the end of a certain period. Most co-operatives are incorporated, for the important reason of protecting the organizers from liability for losses. Also, the corporate status promotes credibility, thus making it easier to sell shares, sign leases, and so forth.

Generally the co-op is nonprofit, and if it is well run so that the books validly show no profits, there will be no tax concerns except giving the information on the tax forms. The Bureau of Internal Revenue scrutinizes quite carefully the distinction between "charitable" and "nonprofit." Since it is unlikely that any food co-operative could be considered legally "charitable," the contributing members would not be able to deduct their contributions from their taxes. Actually, however, the matter of deductions is inconsequential because of the low cost of the shares and the type and value of the return on the investment.

Incidentally, the mark-up on food varies and is usually calculated to run commensurate with the cost of maintaining the business. Often no salaries are paid in the beginning, but if the co-op is to survive with tight organization some recompensation is eventually necessary. We found in the Whole Earth Restaurant that volunteer help was common because of the fun and commitment to the place, but maintaining a prompt and consistent staff required at least a small salary or compensation in steady meals.

Another common method of dispensing food is what is most often termed a "food conspiracy." A food-buying club is organized and memberships sold to each person involved, including children in a family (sometimes there are family memberships). This initial capital enables the club to open a bank account and have a little money for basic purposes such as establishing credit with wholesalers and buying a truck for the food runs. Each week orders are taken in advance of the purchase so that the purchases can be made to correspond as closely to the actual demand as possible. Fluctuations in prices and the possibility of a shortage of a particular food can present certain problems. If the bookkeeping system is efficient, however, each member can be credited or debited accordingly and no one will suffer. The jobs are rotated and each member must contribute time to obtaining and dispensing the food. Overhead is cut considerably by securing a porch, backyard, school, or church as the dispensary so that there is no rent or maintenance. Connections with the wholesalers are made in the initial stages of organization. As expected, no salaries are paid since the responsibilities are divided and rotated, although it is a good idea to give a minimal fee to the bookkeeper because the success and good feelings of the outfit are heavily dependent on accurate accounting. So, for the necessary but small costs of keeping a conspiracy, a slight mark-up in commodities from the wholesale price is inevitable. In some groups, instead of placing a weekly order, each member pays a flat fee, especially in a produce conspiracy. The purchasers then buy all they can with the total amount available that week, and the food is divided up evenly.

One of the most interesting new types of business venture in the United States and Canada is the "direct-charge" co-operative. It is similar to all co-ops in most respects except that *there are no hidden charges.* This means that there is no mark-up on merchandise after the initial price has been established in the negotiations between the co-op buyer and the wholesaler, manufacturer, or farmer. Therefore, pricing in no way provides for the accumulation of capital from the gross margin, and the cost of organizing and maintaining the co-op is met by selling shares and establishing membership fees.

In the beginning, the membership of a direct-charge co-operative should have no less than fifty people if there is to be money to pay rent and establish credit. Sometimes it is necessary to obtain a small loan. A board of directors is appointed and a manager hired. My experience with co-operatives has taught me that, as with a food conspiracy, a small compensation should also be provided for the bookkeeper since it is absolutely necessary that co-op books are kept up to date and open, both for the members and the Internal Revenue Service. As the co-op grows, more paid employees will have to be hired, but this should in no way discourage or inhibit participation by the members.

Generally, a member is required to buy two shares at five dollars each when he or she joins, and to make subsequent purchases of five shares each quarter after the first investment. Then each succeeding year he or she is required to pay twenty dollars (in quarter payments), though no limit should be established in the by-laws as it is difficult to foresee capital needs of the coming years. The share capital is specifically to cover cost of equipment and inventory, rent, initial credit, and future credit needs. Though the budget will be slim in the early stages of the co-op, the continual inflow of money from the quarterly shares corrects shortage in capital. The operating costs of the co-op are met by the weekly charges applied equally to each member. These charges have no relationship to the amount of purchases made by the member. In the beginning they are calculated as a small percentage of the estimated total expenses for a thirteen-week period, the total estimated cost having been divided evenly among all members, and they are collected on a weekly basis. Then after the first quarter, the books will affirm or recommend a change in percentage required for operating the following quarter. An allowance for unforeseen expenses should be calculated into the charges, and at the end of each quarter any surplus, discounts, and rebates will be subtracted from the charges required for the next quarter, as this money is not to be considered capital. In the actual pricing of the commodities themselves, the delivery costs, a fractional mark-up on produce for spoilage, and, of course, sales tax, will have to be taken into account. The need for efficient bookkeeping should be apparent.

My preference for this particular co-operative organization is based upon its sophistication and morality in the financial structure. It demands a solid commitment from the membership. Each member signs a contract that can be terminated with two months' notice, and memberships can be sold back to the co-op or to a new member by anyone who wishes to bow out. Committees are selected from the membership and people are rotated from committee to committee so that they participate in all areas of the business. Selection of merchandise, management, and the physical operation must be agreed upon by the members. If the co-operative sustains itself, it offers much to the community not only as a model, but as a powerful tool in economic democracy. Any person involved in a co-operative organization designed for the dispensation of goods has more control over the economic processes upon which his own life depends. Since we still have many people who are suffering financially, who need guidance in consumerism, the co-op is a great service to the community.

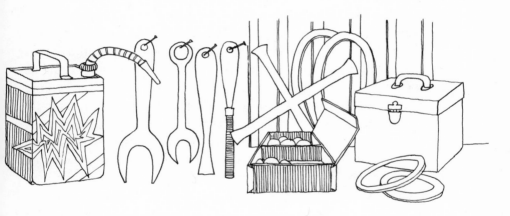

In reality, there are many areas that could benefit from co-operative management, and the degrees of financial and personal involvement vary. For example, one badly needed service in the technological age is a co-operative garage. In some towns in the United States, young people are setting up facilities to cut the costs of maintaining automobiles. In one typical arrangement, a space is obtained for the garage, a business license purchased, and one or two good mechanics offer their skills, which in turn are paid for out of a ten-dollar membership fee and four- to six-dollar monthly dues. All parts are sold at dealer's discount. The members may do their own work if they wish, or they can obtain assistance or even have an entire job done by the mechanics. Other garage co-ops charge an initial fee, eliminate the monthly dues, and charge the member by the hour for the mechanic's labor, or fifty cents an hour for garage fees if the member does his own work. Working hours for the garage depend on the cost of maintaining the co-op. It might be necessary to require the periodic sale of shares. Usually the equipment and tools are purchased from an establishment going out of business, or on credit. When low-income families use these services, it is sometimes possible for that organization to obtain funding from state and federal grants, especially if help is given to older people. One garage co-op in the East has fixed up an old bus to drive aged citizens to receive medical check-ups and treatment.

I think a worthwhile luxury for the emerging community would be to set up a co-operative theater based on the same financial investment policy of a commodity-dispensing co-op. The initial costs of securing a theater and materials for sets and costuming could be met by the membership fees, especially if the members were willing to put some labor into building or fixing the theater. Investors could be paid back in free performances, and a small entrance fee for nonmembers might be directed to paying token wages to the cast and crew. Generally, community theaters are made up of people who are employed elsewhere, but if a theater's financial support were strong enough, there would be possibility for some full-time work.

A community art and/or music center is also a direction for co-operative minds. Studio space is a legitimate dilemma for many artists, now that the housing shortage is so crucial. If such a center were set up as a co-operative, the initial investors could be the artists themselves and the fees could be used to rent or purchase space, and dealer discounts for supplies could be obtained with a business license. Depending on the fees for work, operating costs, and salaries, it might be difficult to continue to maintain the co-operative as a nonprofit business. At some time, then, it could be converted to a profit-making or -sharing corporation, but in the beginning stages when financing is important, the most efficient financial arrangement should be sought. Again, a good accountant or bookkeeper and part-time legal counsel are essential to a co-operative.

Surely the trend toward community co-operatives has an intimacy similar to the small neighborhood businesses of the past century, and would appeal to those who are concerned about the rush to consolidation in the twentieth century. How common it is to hear ourselves mourn the decline of the power of the individual voice in government and commerce. And serious are the reactions of a populace suffering from the emotional isolation of these times. The last few years have proven to me that it is *not* naive and simplistic to consider the "sense of community" a salvation for this corporate century, both in the small business co-operatives where the chances for exploitation and corruption are far less possible, and in the aesthetic recreative projects which offer such therapy through personal expression and interaction.

All kinds of ideas for community involvement are in the air now, some more frivolous than others. For the last two years our town has had a Spring Fair, which is held on the main mall of the commercial section. This event celebrates the work of local artisans, who exhibit their crafts in booths on the street alongside sidewalk tables set up by local storeowners. In addition, music, dance events,

dramatic performances, contests, and food booths are offered. It is profitable for the artists and merchants, of course, and the whole affair has had a unifying and festive effect on the community.

A similar arrangement is the flea market, which is a growing, popular experience all over the country. Many of these are set up in the lots of drive-in theaters, and space is rented to people who bring new and used items to sell or trade. My brother buys all his Christmas and birthday presents at one of the larger flea markets in the San Francisco Bay area. It is a valid act of recycling.

Another community service which interests me is a bimonthly circular put out in our town called "The People's Buy and Sell Press." Anyone who has an item or service (such as handy work, baby-sitting, gardening, and so on) to sell can advertise in the paper and pay a small percentage of the sale price *when the item is sold.* The fees from this arrangement pay the publication costs. The papers themselves are distributed free all over town, and consequently, many more items are put into circulation than ordinarily would be through the classified section of a regular newspaper.

A nice project springing up in the United States and Canada is the community garden. Municipally owned unused pieces of land are divided into plots and rented during the growing season for very small fees. Fees are used to hook into a water line for irrigation and to hire the initial equipment necessary to turn over the earth. In some cities organic fertilizer is donated or purchased by the city. The farmer-renter may elect to raise whatever appeals to his needs or aesthetics and good camaraderie is established among the growers who trade or sell cheaply excess crops to one another. Two or three tenants may plan their sections so they don't duplicate, therefore producing a wider selection of produce. In Canada, private landowners are renting unused land in various-sized plots to city dwellers. Some are even providing camping and recreation areas for the city-dwelling farmers. I remember the victory gardens we kept in Southern California during the Second World War. Our third-grade class even planted a little garden in a corner of the school yard. I moved away from that school before the crops were harvested, but my classmates sent me a letter when they pulled the first turnip from the ground.

Eventually, perhaps, communities will go further with collective-gardening energy and allow citizens with extra time, the old and young and those involved in rehabilitative programs, to take care of parks and municipal landscaping. Space could be allocated to an individual or group who might or might not plant under the direction of the city. Can you imagine what a wonderful patchwork could be created around a city hall?

What to do for and with elderly citizens is a problem facing all communities today. Attempts to create useful occupations for retired people could be expanded into all the areas mentioned so far in this chapter. Along with co-operative stores and community gardening, the energies of the old could be utilized in caring for the young children of working parents. The co-op nursery school is a common institution in American society, but is often short of adult help. For a nation weaned on Red Riding Hood and "to Grandmother's house we go," we have evolved a shocking lack of concern and responsibility for older members of the family and community. The old-age home (and all its unctuous euphemisms—Chateau Retirement Home, Eldercare Convalescent Hospital, Aloha Rest Home) has become a major institution in the United States. True, debilitating illness and the erratic behavior of senility put a severe strain on any family, but I wonder how easy it is for us to classify the set ways that seem to come with age as a form of lapsing mentality. At any rate, even a partial reorganization of activities for older people would benefit everyone. Why could we not have these people working in the less strenuous area of recycling and ecology action centers and any of the other volunteer agencies for community improvement?

The key to the success of working with older people is working toward the return to an age-integrated society. For too long we have compartmentalized the stages of life and isolated ourselves from ourselves in time. If longevity continues to increase, we need to

207

accept the elderly more humanely. Especially now, when there is a return to crafts and the resourceful know-how of the past, the community should foster the opportunity for the older to teach the younger. Think of the expertise in quilting, crocheting, embroidery, knitting. Older people should be loosely included in all expositions of talent and in areas of entertainment. Years ago, when my son was very young and taking afternoon naps, I would sit on the deck of our house and listen to the old woman next door read Shakespeare under a trellis in the corner of her garden. My love of this small program has stayed with me through the years and I wish there had been other places in the community, like a co-operative theater, where she could have been appreciated.

It's obvious, when one tosses around ideas for bringing the community together, that the possibilities are rich. On a smaller scale, neighborhoods everywhere could set up their own exchanges for goods and services in a small area. Bulletin boards in laundromats and markets are good places for advertising. Participants could trade professional repairs and talents in return for specific wants or bids. In fact, money exchange might be eliminated entirely.

The days when you could trade half a hog for a bolt of cloth at the local dry goods store no longer exist. Hardly a grocery store in the country sells on credit anymore or even delivers its commodities. The old-time family cooperation within the small town community is history except for the various, not yet really numerous, examples of cooperative movements. I believe that even a limited revival of community activity and spirit will do much to offset the hard edge of our technological society.

ADDITIONAL READING

Griffin, Al. *How to Start and Operate a Day Care Center.* Chicago: Henry Regnery Company.
Somewhere Else—A living, learning catalog (edited by The Center for Curriculum Design with a Foreword by John Holt). Chicago: The Swallow Press, Inc.

CHAPTER 10

The Restoration of Ritual

I believe in the essential sanity of man, and

what follows is a memorial to that belief.

JOHN FOWLES, *The Aristos*

IN THE VERY late part of the afternoon of every working day since I started this book, it has become my custom to turn away from my desk to face a window that overlooks the ocean. One day as I was looking out and gathering thoughts for this chapter, which is about rituals, it occurred to me that I was actually observing a ritual, and that I had created it for myself. I realized that I had established this pause in my day for rest and reflection, and because it was the time of day I could look at the ocean without the sun's glare. The horizon is defined and still, and the outside activity of the day is almost over. It's "the poet's time of day," someone once said. As the Fall moved in I adjusted my ritual to the shorter days. The realization that this moment had become a part of my life and that I needed it to sort out my mind, is what moves me to consider it a ritual.

Rituals, as we traditionally define them, are acts or rites growing out of years, or even generations, of common beliefs and customs. We think of them as ceremonies to observe religious faith, birth, marriage, death; as experiences to commemorate past privation and hard times; and as festivities that memorialize the times of good fortune—all acts that hold a society or a family together. A historical period and the social, economic, and cultural value of the time can be identified by the nature of a ritual. The decline of established rituals is generally an indication of uncertainty and transformation of a social

211

order. I think that in this century and in this society, we can attribute the disappearance of many rituals not only to changing values, but to the usurpation of communication by technological devices. The availability of telephones, television, movies, and rapid transportation has removed the novelty and excitement from the act of people coming together.

I suggest that we reconstruct our definition of rituals to celebrate small events and everyday acts that we have always dismissed as habits or customs, and to give new tribute to those traditional rituals that have lost their meaning by being separated from belief over the years. I'd like to think that our devotion to and belief in a ritual derive from the feeling that what we are honoring is real and good. A ritual should bring forth in us, whether we are alone or with others, special feelings of contentment, of laughter, of hope, and of communication with and respect for all living things. In essence, it affirms and reinforces the interdependency of person and spirit, person and nature, person and person.

In the world today, a profound change has taken place in most religious institutions as well as in attitudes toward religion. In our society, the young generation is turning to organized religion in part as an atonement for the years when religious experiences were not a part of their lives. Such is the swing of the sociological pendulum. I see the most significant and contributory change in religious activity in the redefinition of the relationship between church and state. Many religious leaders, who were concerned in the past with spiritual matters applicable in a practical sense only in a vague, allegorical way, are restructuring their roles to cope with the moral and ethical problems of a modern world. As a result, in many churches rituals that have traditionally concentrated on spiritual needs are recognizing human needs.

Attitudes toward population and birth in these times are curious. It seems that as concern about the increasing population grows, so does the concern over each individual birth. There is no question that the world's population is growing. As long as the death rate remains lower than the birth rate, the population is on the increase. So much has been published in the last few years about the effects of the population boom that we are witnessing what might be considered a backlash of reverence for birth among the younger generation. Actually, I believe the correlation is not direct, but that this new phenomenon is more a reaction to the total picture of the impersonal technological times.

Today's views of birth vary from that of a routine event to one of a ritual of deep mystical experience. The interesting and important change is the consciousness of the woman during the act of birth. The preference for natural childbirth has gained so much support that many major hospitals consider it routine and many obstetricians encourage their patients to attend classes to learn the techniques of experiencing birth without drugs and anesthesia. The whole process of giving birth, then, becomes a ritual practiced during the preceding months. The desire for this experience along with the concern over the impersonal quality in hospital procedure is more often the reason for the increase in home births than the prohibitive cost of hospitalization. The midwife's traditional patience with the natural timing of the birth becomes preferable to the doctor's hectic schedule. These comments are not necessarily a cry for home births, but more of a plea for an understanding of why this new social pattern has developed. The idea that birth can become a ritual, too, is an unquestionable consequence of the general movement toward humanizing our personal histories.

If we think attitudes toward birth are changing, consider the course of marriage in the last ten years. I am not concerned here with analyzing the institution. The expansion of the events of the ceremony, however, is a reflection of the general changes toward the nature and quality of marriage itself. A justifiable wish to make the ritual an aesthetic overture to the lifestyle that will follow has somewhat displaced the traditional wedding ceremony. Young people are reconstructing the ceremony and planning the whole day to include the friends, music, physical setting, food, and entertainment that they love. I regard these very personal celebrations as an obvious indication of respect for and belief in marriage.

In our society, death is as much a business deal as are birth and marriage—only much darker. A lot has been written about the American way of dealing with death, but I think it is one force in our culture that still needs reevaluation. Though longevity continues to increase, so does the number of degenerative ailments peculiar to the technological society. This may be why death is so difficult for us; it takes so long to die. The ritual of memorializing a life becomes unpleasantly complicated with American funeral practices. I find it surreal to offer suggestions for death rituals, but I submit that the grandfather in the movie, *Little Big Man*, may have been on the track. American Indians have always surrounded death with the life force instead of the false sobriety American whites have evolved.

So far, I have mentioned the traditional major events to which we attach the acts of ritual. I am not suggesting specific alternatives; only that the option to redesign rites honoring these occasions belongs to the persons involved. My real concern here is with the smaller events that we conventionally regard as customs.

When I think of rituals in my own life, I begin by remembering occasions from my childhood. For many years after church we ate Sunday dinner out. It was, of course, a special event because taking four children out to eat was no small financial matter even in those early postwar days. The ritual went on for many years, and I loved it—with everyone catering to my little sister in her high chair so she wouldn't disturb the restaurant. I always ordered shrimp; in fact after a time I was afraid not to, for fear an alternative would not be as good and I would wish I had ordered the shrimp. My brother did the same thing. He probably still orders it. Because we ate this big meal in the early afternoon, we had a light supper. My mother often tried to institute a bread and milk supper, which was the Sunday evening ritual of her childhood, but we voted it down each time.

Something that was, and still is, an important part of our

Christmas Eve is supper, with its principle dish of Norwegian meatballs. The recipe dates from my father's childhood, and my mother made them faithfully every Christmas Eve. My older sister still makes them each Christmas since she cooks them best of all. Every time I smell meatballs on Christmas Eve, I remember small things from many years back.

Christmas is conventionally a time for rituals. Almost everyone has something familiar and consistent to integrate into the festivities, although the modern pace has, for many, eliminated a lot of fun rituals from the holidays, such as the making of traditional foods, decorations, and gifts. It's good to see young families returning to the celebration of small things at Christmas time. Several years ago I spent a great deal of time with a young couple and their two small children. The father was an uncommonly talented artist, though they were always poor. One Christmas he gave us a card that was also a tree ornament. It is a beautiful decoration, and I still put it on our tree each year. As luck would have it, they are still poor, but their children never suffer for creative ideas or the rituals of creativity.

215

Another family that I have had the honor to know observes a Christmas tradition that is worth incorporating into one's own holiday. The father reads Dylan Thomas's *A Child's Christmas in Wales* as part of the Christmas Eve ritual. The practice of reading and telling stories aloud is neglected in our time because of the availability of television. Reading stories in a family group is a ritual that should be brought back into American life, not only for entertainment and expression, but for the sheer cohesive reinforcement of the group. Let us consider also the fun and importance of passing on family stories which, since they will never be written down, will otherwise eventually be forgotten. Story telling was once *the* form of entertainment and *the* method of imparting ethics, values, and history, but so many great yarns have turned into dust on the television set. In spite of the visual orientation that has become so prevalent among us since the Second World War, there are hardly any children or adults today that do not still like to hear a story told to *them*. As children, we looked forward to the weekly story hour at the local library, and it was *always* an exercise for our visual imagination.

The everyday meal hour has become a problem of wide concern lately, and we desperately need to redesign this time together. The evening sit-down meal is a perfect time to bring the family or living group together for reorientation and communication, although it need not be only in the evening. It's the sitting down together that is important. A moment of pause before, a leisurely meal of conversation (argue if you wish), and another moment of pause after. There is no time in the day more unifying.

My close friend of many years, Jeanne Houston, gave me more thoughts about meals. In *Farewell to Manzanar*, the story of her years in the California Japanese detention camp during the Second World War, she describes the meals in the camp. Everyone stood in line, cafeteria style, to be served, and each person could sit where he or she wanted. Under the strained circumstances of the incarceration, families found it difficult to sit together, as it was necessary to mingle

216

socially in order to live successfully with so many others in such limited space. Jeanne was the youngest of ten children and cherished the ritual of the family meal. She saw the imposed meal structure as a contributing force in the breakdown of traditional Japanese family life. To this day she will put together every table available in the neighborhood before she capitulates to a buffet. She does create wonderful occasions with her sense of companionship. We frequently have a late Sunday morning brunch at the Houstons' house with lots of garden-grown food, guests, and champagne. The meal lasts for hours and the stories fly all afternoon.

An old Yankee tradition is the taking of food gifts when invited for a meal. The bringing of a bottle of wine is now customary, but I love it when someone brings bread, jam, or relish. Not only can you take presents when you are invited to someone's house, but it's a good opportunity to recycle treasured items, aesthetic or amusing. It's the gesture of contribution, of remembrance, that makes the communication. My two sisters and my brother and I all live in the same county and see each other almost daily. Over the years we have developed a ritual of bringing something, anything, to one another when we visit. My brother is the chief of originality in this, as he frequents flea markets so much and finds incredible stuff. Recently he brought me a pair of work boots made in Missouri in 1906. They had leather tops with two-inch pine soles. I gave them back the next time I went to visit. After all, one needn't always take this ritual seriously.

It is an unfortunate truth that we have lost information about many traditions in our culture, not only because of the advance of technical communication, but also because of the almost pathological obsession of many foreign-born to become "American." I'd like to see us make up our own occasions and develop our own rituals to complement and enrich them. Already many younger people are celebrating events and occasions heretofore forgotten except by anthropologists, like the phases of the moon, medieval fairs and old-time bazaars, and community market days. It's called the "make-your-own-event" era, with a sliding scale of size and sophistication.

At the Whole Earth Restaurant we designated the birthday of anyone on the staff to be the major event to celebrate as a working group, and, because we had a lot of people, we had a good excuse to party often. I have always been a devotee of the birthday, and to this day neither my sisters, my brother, nor I would think of letting a birthday go by without a party with all attending. When we were children it was *the* day we could choose anything we wanted for dinner. At the restaurant the parties were always surprises, even if we had to have them on days other than the actual birthdays. Champagne was a ritual, as was a big, not overly healthful cake. The rest of the act depended on the nature of the person and the time of year.

The most telling commentary on this birthday fixation of mine came from Jane, who had worked with me since the opening of the restaurant. She said, "You know, Sharon, when I awoke this morning and became conscious of the fact that it was your birthday, I wondered if I should remember it every minute or could I forget once in a while during the day." Although my own fondness of birthdays may be considered excessive by some, I do think that we may tend to dismiss the birthday as a product of the material age, when it is really a fine occasion for all good friends to celebrate existence. It doesn't have to be expensive; make it potluck, a picnic—it's yours to design!

How many still involve themselves in the annual family reunion? Or have the children grown up and away, vowing not to go to those boring occasions? With the attitudes as they are, most parents would be surprised to see their children opt for the event. When I remember these discontinued occasions, I laugh and cry at the differences, gaps, and similarities. I loved them as a child, but, as in most American families, the cousins have scattered and the elders are "getting on." *Bring back the family reunion* is a campaign worth considering. Because my mother's immediate family is scattered throughout the country, her brothers and sisters, seven in all, have circulated a continual family letter for the last thirty years. Each time you receive the letter you are, within a week or so, to remove your own previous contribution to the letter and write another in its place. I have always thought of this as a beautiful ritual of communication.

So, make your own rituals. I can think of many ideas for occasions and ceremonies we have tossed around in our own community. In the restaurant, we talked of tea on the deck at sunset, and breakfast on the beach at sunrise. We did celebrate the graduation of any restaurant staff member with a potluck breakfast for all that graduate's friends and family along with the restaurant family. And it will probably become a ritual to rank with the birthday.

Living by the beach makes it easy to change habits into customs and customs into rituals: morning runs, sunset walks, supper picnics, and the Fourth of July beach party. Perhaps it explains my devotion to my afternoon ocean watch. My street to the sea is a dead end and whoever walks down must come back. It's a ritual of familiar faces and familiar habits. Those moments that are constant, familiar, and low-keyed—as well as the special, more elaborate occasions of pageantry—preserve our essential sanity.

In Mexico, we would walk up in the hills behind the village where we lived, find a spot, and watch the sun set in those spectacular, clear skies, seven thousand feet higher than I am today. I thought then that I would never know that sort of peace anywhere else, but I have, and I am sure that I will find it in many places if I look for it.

Index

221

locks 73–76
of beer 79
of wine 70, 73, 76–77
Fermenter
winemaking equipment 71–72
sugar as, in wine 70, 73
Fertilizer
fish emulsion 10, 23, 27
homemade mix 29
mulching 29; compost 184
using 23
Freezing 39, 42–46
fruits 42–43, 46, 52
vegetables 39, 42–45
Frozen foods, shopping for 150–151
fish 153
vegetables 151
Fruit
canning 34, 35–38, 41–42
drying 46–47
freezing 42–43, 46, 52;
using frozen fruit 46, 52
jams, jellies, conserves, etc.
48–65; see also Recipes
syrup 54
wines 67–77; recipes 70–71
Fruit types:
Apples
canning 41
freezing 46
pectin 49, 50; recipe 50–51
recipes: apple butter 52
chutney, apple and tomato 57
vinegars 63–65
Apricots
canning 38, 42
freezing 46
wine, recipe 70
Bananas, shopping for 155
Berries
canning 38, 42
freezing 46
jams, etc. 50

Blackberries
canning 42; see also Berries
freezing 46; see also Berries
wine, recipe 71
Cantaloupe and plum conserve,
recipe 55
Cherries
canning 38, 42
jams, etc. 50
wine, recipe 71
Citrus fruits
seeds, for house plants 11
shopping for 155
see also Oranges
Cranberry sauce, recipe 54
Fig jam, recipe 52
Grapes
recipes: conserve 56
jelly 51
vinegar 63
wines 69–70, 73–74
Muskmelon, see Cantaloupe and plum
conserve, recipe
Oranges
freezing 46
seeds, for house plants 11
Peaches
canning 38, 42
freezing 46
jams, etc. 50
recipe, chutney 56–57
Pears
canning 38, 42
freezing 46
jams, etc. 50
vinegar, recipe 64
Persimmons
persimmon butter, recipe 53
serving 52
Pineapples, canning 42
Plums
canning 42
freezing 46